Neil J. Anderson

ACTIVE
Skills for **Reading**: Book 2

Nancy Hubley

Teacher's Guide

THOMSON

HEINLE

Australia · Canada · Mexico · Singapore · Spain · United Kingdom · United States

THOMSON

HEINLE

Active Skills for Reading, 2nd Edition, Teacher's Guide 2

Anderson / Hubley

Editorial Director: Joe Dougherty
VP, Director of Content Development: Anita Raducanu
Director of Product Marketing: Amy Mabley
Director of Global Field Marketing: Ian Martin
Editorial Manager: Sean Bermingham
Development Editor: Derek Mackrell
Content Project Manager: Tan Jin Hock

Sr. Print Buyer: Mary Beth Hennebury
Contributing Writer: Nancy Hubley
Contributing Editor: Colleen Sheils
Compositor: CHROME Media Pte. Ltd. / C. Hanzie
Cover/Text Designer: CHROME Media Pte. Ltd.
Printer: West Group

For more information contact Thomson Heinle, 25 Thomson Place, Boston, Massachusetts 02210 USA. You can visit our web site at elt.heinle.com

For permission to use material from this text or product, submit a request online at http://www.thomsonrights.com Any additional questions about permissions can be submitted by e-mail to thomsonrights@thomson.com

ISBN-13: 978-1-4240-0209-2
ISBN-10: 1-4240-0209-5

Contents

Over the years I have been fortunate to be able to meet and train a wide variety of EFL/ESL reading instructors from many places around the world. All reading instructors recognize that the teaching of good reading skills and strategies is a vital part of learners' English development.

In my discussions with these teachers, certain questions have come up a number of times. In the following list of frequently asked questions, I have provided some answers to these common concerns.

Neil J. Anderson

"It's sometimes difficult to get my students motivated to read in English. How can this book help?"

I understand exactly how you feel. I face that same challenge in my classes. Motivation can come from outside the reader (external motivation) as well as inside the reader (internal motivation). I work hard to make sure that I am providing the appropriate external motivations so that my students will want to be in class and will want to try to improve their reading.

ACTIVE Skills for Reading uses high-interest texts relevant to students' lives and interests. For example, there are readings on studying abroad, money and budgets, use of the Internet, and cross-cultural topics. In the second edition, I have included a wider variety of text types. Students will get practice reading interviews, diary extracts, and recipes, as well as articles—the kinds of reading materials they'll face in real life. I find that these text types, in combination with the topics, really help to motivate readers.

"My students want to read in English but they think it's too difficult. How can this book help?"

Sometimes students get discouraged because they are reading a book that is too difficult. There are five books in this series. The passages in each of these books are carefully graded to the appropriate level. The passages here are designed so that they are not too long and that they incorporate suitable vocabulary and grammar. I encourage teachers to select the appropriate level of book from the series so that they will be able to engage their students appropriately. Furthermore, an Intro level has been added to meet the needs of beginning level readers.

"What should I do before I have students read the passage?"

Engaging students in prereading activities is an essential part of getting them motivated to read more. If we fail to prepare them well, they will not be meaningfully engaged while reading. Each unit begins with the *Get Ready* section with thought-provoking questions to activate the students' prior knowledge (the *A* in ACTIVE Reading). Each chapter begins with a *Before You Read* section that also provides an opportunity for the reader to link what they already know with what they are about to read.

"My students struggle with reading because they find so many unfamiliar words. How can this book help them deal with vocabulary?"

Vocabulary knowledge is essential for successful reading. The *C* in ACTIVE Reading focuses specifically on cultivating vocabulary. Two successful features from the first edition of the series are the vocabulary comprehension and vocabulary skill sections.

I have included a vocabulary index at the back of the student book to help both the teacher and the students. I have also added eight vocabulary learning tips to help readers be focused in how they approach vocabulary study. Review these tips on pages 6–7. I've added a list of common prefixes and suffixes in order to help readers focus on word analysis skills.

Together, these sections will help your students successfully address their vocabulary learning needs.

"Sometimes my students understand the words in a passage, but they don't really understand the overall meaning. How can I help my students to really comprehend the meaning of a text?"

This is an excellent opportunity for you to help your students see that successful reading is more than knowing the meanings of individual words. To be a successful reader, students must move to understanding the overall meaning of what they are reading. After each reading passage, *ACTIVE Skills for Reading* provides reading comprehension questions that cover a range of comprehension skills from literal (facts and main ideas) to more inferential.

We have also added *Critical Thinking* questions to encourage students to use their own opinions and thoughts to relate to the ideas in the texts. These sections of the book are designed to get the readers to think about meaning, the *T* in ACTIVE. Those who used the first edition will notice that the T has changed from "teach for comprehension" to "think about meaning." This is because I want to provide the readers with more opportunities to think about meaning and monitor their own comprehension.

"My students often take a long time to read a text in English, which discourages them. How can I get them to read more fluently?"

Fluent reading is the area that interests me the most about teaching reading. I know that most second language readers read more slowly in their second language than in their first. This is a matter that must be directly addressed by teachers. We cannot ignore the explicit teaching of fluent reading.

Twelve tips for fluent reading are provided on pages 8–9 of the student book. As well, the Review Units provide explicit practice in developing readers' reading rates. Specific instructions on how to use rate building activities in the classroom are addressed on pages 10–11. Have your students record their progress using the charts at the back of the book. Those charts have become a great source of motivation for my students for improving their reading fluency.

"I'm worried that my students might try a reading strategy once, then forget about it. How can I encourage them to really develop their strategy use?"

I keep a list of the key reading skills taught in each chapter in the classroom and encourage students to report how they are using them outside of the classroom. These key reading skills are recycled through each book, and across the series (predicting, main ideas, scanning, etc), so that students get multiple opportunities to practice them.

New to this edition are other strategy techniques, presented in the Review Units— see above and below, which students can use in any type of reading. The Review Units also provide a *Self Check* section to help readers focus on how to transfer the use of the strategies from in-class reading to all their reading opportunities.

"How can I tell whether my students are making progress in their reading?"

The *E* in *ACTIVE* reminds us to evaluate progress. Making learners aware of their progress ties into their motivation to continue learning to be good readers. One way this is done in *ACTIVE Skills for Reading* is quantitatively. Readers can get a "score" on the comprehension questions and the vocabulary questions. Monitoring reading rate through the use of the charts is another progress marker.

In addition to the quantitative progress markers, there are qualitative markers as well. Responses to the *Critical Thinking* and the *What Do You Think?* questions provide progress markers. Teachers can use the question bank on the ExamView® assessment CD-ROM to create progress tests, or mid-book and final exams.

"Many of my students are planning to take a standardized exam in the future, such as TOEFL®, TOEIC®, or IELTS. How can this course help them prepare?"

All of the reading skills covered in *ACTIVE Skills for Reading* are useful for standardized examinations. Strong reading skills are essential for any of the standardized exams. Reading rate development will help students deal with the time limits in the exam. ExamView® includes question formats that appear in standardized exams like TOEFL®

iBT and IELTS.* The ASR website also gives additional quizzes to develop vocabulary.

"There's only so much I can do with my students during class time. How can I encourage them to read more outside of class?"

We should encourage our students to take responsibility for their own development as readers by encouraging them to read as much as they can outside of class. The Internet is an excellent resource for extensive reading. The ASR website elt.thomson.com/asr includes guided search activities that allow students to build on what they are learning from the readings in the book.

The *Real Life Skill* section of the coursebook gives guidance on dealing with Internet research and blogs as well as other contexts. This section acts as a bridge between the coursebook and out-of-class reading.

I also encourage students to use graded readers. The Thomson Heinle *Foundations Readers* and *Footprint Readers* series, for example, are excellent resources that students could turn to for appropriate reading material. As students become better readers they will be better language learners.

* See page 64 for an overview of the TOEFL® iBT
  reading skills covered in *ACTIVE Skills for Reading Book 2*.

Unit Walkthrough

Getting Ready

Each unit begins with the section *Getting Ready*, with visual prompts in the form of photos or illustrations, and discussion questions, or a survey, all related to the unit topic. The aim of this section is to *activate* students' prior understanding, or background knowledge, about the unit topic. Many of the questions are designed so students will personalize the topic and bring their own real-life experiences into the classroom.

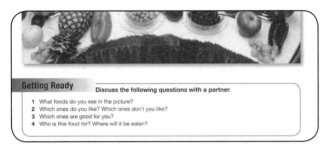

In the Classroom

As the teacher, if you feel that the *Getting Ready* questions are not relevant to your students' cultural environment or learning situation, feel free to write your own questions. Try not to skip over this section, but rather, prepare an activity that will meet the needs of your students. Remember that questions in this section should get students thinking about the overall unit topic. If your students' vocabulary skill level is low, think about introducing topic-related questions or activities that encourage students to generate more vocabulary.

Chapters 1 & 2
Before You Read

Every unit of the book has two chapters and each chapter begins with a section entitled *Before You Read*. This section contains a series of questions to *activate* students' background knowledge about each chapter's reading. This is done in various ways. Sometimes students must analyze how vocabulary in the reading relates to the topic. Other times, students must use the title of the reading passage to make guesses about factual content or vocabulary they are likely to encounter. These tasks serve to cultivate students' vocabulary before they read, and the activation of background knowledge gives students a more successful reading experience.

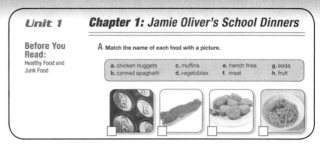

In the Classroom

As the teacher, you can supplement the *Before You Read* sections in both chapters with activities you feel will help prepare students for success with the reading. Some examples include activities that are vocabulary based, discussion based, or a combination of both. Feel free to develop your own activities based on those already provided in the text.

Reading Skill

Each chapter of *ACTIVE Skills for Reading, 2nd Edition* teaches a reading strategy, so there are two strategies in every unit. With guidance from the text, as well as the teacher, students will learn to use strategies including predicting, scanning, using subtitles to predict content, skimming for main ideas, identifying transition words, making inferences, recognizing sequence of events, identifying main ideas, distinguishing main ideas and supporting details, identifying main ideas within paragraphs, and identifying cause and effect.

These strategies aim to show students how to approach reading in a more fluent, native-reader manner. Note that many of the strategies appear more than once throughout the book. Through repeated practice, students will become skilled in each strategy. Hence this section is entitled *Reading Skill*.

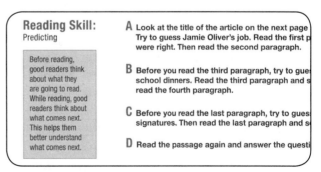

In the Classroom

Each *Reading Skill* section contains a box that describes a reading skill and explains how to utilize it. Make sure students read this box before they complete the *Reading Skill* activity. If students struggle to understand the explanation and instructions, help them by providing more details or by modeling the skill. This will help students *verify* the *strategies* they are learning, and guide them in developing their reading skills.

All readings in Book 2 are approximately 400 words long. Each line is numbered so students can easily ask about items in the reading and teachers can more effectively answer any questions about content.

day in theaters everywhere. Set in a village outside London
d of World War II, the movie tells the story of a woman living
se visited by ghosts from the war. The movie is based on the   5
e Haunting of Powell Manor by Robert Johnston.
eally impressed," said moviegoer Diana Owens of Los
"It's a ghost story that will keep you guessing and jumping.
oint, a scene in the movie was so scary that *everyone* in the
creamed." There's also a surprise ending to the story. "I   10
I you what it is," said Owens, "but pay attention to the word

Most readings also have footnotes. These sometimes contain references to geographical locations mentioned in the text, which are also referenced in the maps in the back of the book. Topic-specific vocabulary items, as well as lower frequency vocabulary fundamental to the overall understanding of the reading, are often footnoted. Pronunciation of difficult words is also footnoted, as are explanatory notes on historical references in the text.

¹**Feed Me Better website** www.feedmebetter.com
²**signature** a name at the end of a document, usually handwritten, e.g. *Roger Morton*
³**prime minister** the leader of the government in some countries, e.g., Japan, Australia, the U.K.

Reading Comprehension

Every chapter has a *Reading Comprehension* section that consists of three parts. Part A has four comprehension questions. Part B involves an additional comprehension check. Part C consists of critical thinking questions to encourage readers to move beyond the text and begin applying information that they are reading in a critical way. Numerous task types are presented such as identifying true or false statements, sentence correction, statement completion, and multiple-choice questions.

The aim of the *Reading Comprehension* section is to teach students how to *think about meaning* as well as test their ability to comprehend. This section practices the reading skills—identifying main ideas, scanning, and skimming—which all contribute to comprehension of the text.

Reading Comprehension: Check Your Understanding

A The statements below are about the reading. Choose the correct answ to complete each one.

1 Jamie Oliver is a _____.
   a. prime minister   b. student   c. chef
2 Oliver thinks that _____ is junk food.
   a. meat   b. canned spaghetti   c. fruit

In the Classroom

While completing these exercises, students should try not to look back at the reading passage for the answers. However, if their reading is generally slow, allow them to scan through the reading to find the correct answers. After students have answered the questions, have them compare their answers in pairs or groups. Students should show each other where to find the answers in the passage. If your teaching situation permits, go over this exercise with students as a class. If you think students need more practice, create more comprehension questions based on the task type used in the chapter.

Vocabulary Comprehension

In every chapter there is a *Vocabulary Comprehension* section, divided into two parts. Eight vocabulary items from each reading have been identified as key words that students at this level should analyze and learn in order to expand their core vocabulary. In Part A, different task types are presented, such as matching vocabulary items to correct definitions, identifying the odd word out in a sequence, and recognizing the meaning of words in context. All of the vocabulary items have been italicized to make them more easily identifiable within the exercises.

In Part B of the *Vocabulary Comprehension* exercise, students practice using four of the key vocabulary items from Part A in alternative contexts by completing cloze sentences, gap-fill activities, or giving alternative examples to illustrate their understanding of meaning and nuance.

Both parts of the Vocabulary Comprehension section aim to assist students in further *cultivating* a rich *vocabulary*.

Vocabulary Comprehension: Words in Context

A The words in *italics* are vocabulary items from the reading. Read each question or statement and choose the best answer. Check your answers with a partner.

1 *Simple* foods are usually _____.
   a. easy to make   b. difficult to make
2 Does your school serve _____?

In the Classroom

In addition to the exercises in the text, you may supplement this activity by having students give other examples of the vocabulary items in context, or by having them write sentences using all or some of the vocabulary items. Not all of the vocabulary items in the exercise will be new to all students; there may also be passive vocabulary items in the reading passage that students are encountering for the first time. An alternative exercise would be for students to choose five vocabulary items from the passage that are new to them, and use those words in sentences. Allow students time to share their sentences with a partner, or as a group, and encourage peer correction. If there is not enough class time to do this, assign it as homework.

Vocabulary Skill

In every chapter there is a *Vocabulary Skill* section. This is designed to teach strategies that will help students improve their capacity to learn and comprehend new vocabulary items. These strategies include creating word webs, using synonyms and antonyms, recognizing root words, using prefixes and suffixes, organizing vocabulary into topical contexts, analyzing adjective and noun endings, using compound nouns and adjectives, using phrasal verbs, and understanding word families.

Often the vocabulary items in the Vocabulary Skill exercises come from the reading passage. This helps students revise, recycle, and further cultivate vocabulary as well as shows students how these strategies may be used in a broader linguistic framework. In this sense, this section aims to increase students' metacognitive awareness of the process of building transferable vocabulary skills, which in turn allows them to *verify* their own reading *strategies*.

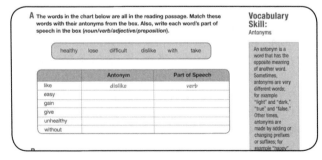

In the Classroom

Depending on your students' vocabulary levels, you may want to make this section more challenging by adding additional vocabulary to the exercise. Feel free to create your own activities based on those in the text. In addition, or as an alternative to the above, you may want to assign extra writing activities. Have students use some, or all, of the vocabulary in this section to write sentences of their own. If there is no class time for this, assign it as homework. If students are asked to give alternative examples of the vocabulary items, make sure to have them discuss their ideas in pairs or, if your teaching situation permits, small groups. If there is enough time, call on students to share their ideas with the class.

Real Life Skill & What Do You Think?

Real Life Skill

On the final page of each unit is the *Real Life Skill* section, which aims to develop students' reading and comprehension skills using a variety of realia. Examples of such materials include visitor arrival forms, movie reviews, telephone directories, newspaper articles, and dictionary entries.

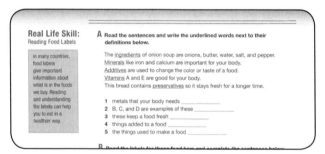

In the Classroom

Every *Real Life Skill* section contains a box that gives information and guidance on developing a skill. Make sure students read this skill box before they start the activity. Reading the skill boxes will enable students to *verify* the *strategies* they are learning, and guide them in developing their reading skills.

Allow students to work in pairs to complete the exercise. If necessary, students can, and should, use their dictionaries for help. If this exercise cannot be completed during class time, have students finish it as homework

What Do You Think?

Each unit ends with the section *What Do You Think?* Consisting of discussion questions, the aim of this section is to get students to share their ideas and opinions about the reading topics, and to discuss in more detail the issues raised in the readings from both chapters. Many of the questions allow students to personalize the reading topics, giving students the opportunity again to bring their own real-life experiences into the classroom.

Using the Audio Component

With every level of the second edition of ACTIVE Skills for Reading, there is an audio component on cassette or CD, which consists of recordings of the reading passages in the book. Using the audio can benefit both teachers and students: Non-native English teachers, for example, may wish to listen for correct pronunciation and intonation of vocabulary items and expressions in the reading. For students, the audio allows them to hear how vocabulary and expressions in the reading are spoken by a native English speaker.

Please note, however, that the passages have been recorded by native English speakers, at near native English speed. These recordings are not designed to be used for listening comprehension exercises in class, but rather as a way of attuning students' ears to the sound of native-spoken English. Students can be encouraged to build their reading fluency by listening to the CD while they read, and trying to keep the same pace as the recording. This will give them additional practice to increase their reading rate.

Review Units

After every three units there is a *Review Unit*. There are two primary purposes of the *Review Unit*. First, to provide practice in the development of *reading fluency* and second, to allow readers to review the vocabulary taught in the earlier three units.

Every *Review Unit* contains a *Fluency Strategy* box that contains information on the strategy for that unit, and gives students guidance on how to develop and use it. Make sure students read this strategy box before they start the activity. The reading passage then provides explicit practice of the fluency strategy.

Fluency Strategy: *SQ3R*

SQ3R is a simple way to help you be a better, more fluent reader and to increase your reading comprehension. SQ3R stands for Survey, Question, Read, Review, Recite.

First Reading

There are three readings in each *Review Unit*. The first reading focuses on explicit instruction of a specific fluency strategy. PRO, PQR+E, KWL, and Reading ACTIVEly are addressed in Book 2.

Self Check

After the first reading passage, there is a *Self Check*, which gives an opportunity for students to reflect on their experience using the fluency strategy taught in that *Review Unit*.

Second and Third Reading Passages

The primary focus for the second and third reading passages in each *Review Unit* is to build up reading fluency. To help students *increase reading fluency*, use activities such as Rate Build-up, Repeated Reading, or Class-paced Reading for the second passage. For the third passage, students should be encouraged to use Self-paced Reading. These specific activities for building reading rate are described below.

Four Activities for Building Reading Rate

To help students increase their reading rate, consider using one of the following activities.

1. Rate Build-up Drill

Students are given sixty seconds to read as much material as they can. After the first sixty-second period ends, they start reading again from the beginning of the text for an additional sixty seconds. This drill is repeated a third and a fourth time. Students should be able to reread the "old" material faster and faster, extending into new material. By the end of the activity, students should be reading more material in the last sixty-second period than in the first. As students repeat this rate-building activity, their reading rate should increase. After four sixty-second periods, encourage students to continue reading the passage through to the end.

2. Repeated Reading

Students read a short passage over and over until they achieve criterion levels of reading rate and comprehension. For example, they may try to read a short 75-word paragraph three times in two minutes. The criterion levels may vary from class to class, but reasonable goals to work toward are criterion levels of 100 words per minute at 70% comprehension. After conducting this repeated reading activity, ask students to read the entire passage and then do the exercises.

3. Class-paced Reading

This activity requires establishing a class goal for a minimal reading rate. Once that goal is established, the average number of words per page or paragraph of the material being read must be calculated. Then how much material needs to be read in one minute to meet the class goal should be determined. For example, if the class goal is to read 100 words per minute and the material being read has an average of 50 words per paragraph, the class would be expected to read one paragraph every thirty seconds. As each thirty-second period elapses, the teacher signals for the class to move to the next paragraph. Students are encouraged to keep up with the established class goal. Of course, those who read faster than 100 words per minute are not expected to reduce their reading rate. As long as they are ahead of the designated paragraph or page they should continue reading. As part of the class-paced reading activity, one suggestion is to play the audio CD that accompanies this book and have students follow along. This would provide practice in reading fluency at the rate of the native speaker on the CD.

4. Self-paced Reading

A class goal for reading fluency can be established, such as 100 words per minute. Students can either time themselves or, if they do not have a watch with a second hand, the teacher could use a watch or clock to keep time progress on the board for the class goal. All students must start reading at the same time. When students are finished, they must look up at the board in the classroom for the time or check a watch. As students are reading, write the passing time on the board at fifteen-second intervals. Start the count after students have been reading for one minute. When students have finished reading, they should look at the most recent time recorded on the board and use it to enter their reading rate in the chart on page 176.

Reading Rate Chart

Time (minutes)	Review Reading								Rate (words per minute)
	1	2	3	4	5	6	7	8	
1:00									400
1:15									320
1:30									267
1:45									229
2:00									200
2:15									178
2:30									160

Reading Comprehension

After the second and the third reading passages in the *Review Unit*, there are *Reading Comprehension* sections. Each *Reading Comprehension* section consists of seven multiple-choice questions. The aim of this section is to teach students how to *think about meaning* as well as test their ability to comprehend. Comprehension also comes about by practicing reading skills such as identifying main ideas, scanning, and skimming.

Reading Comprehension

1 Why did the writer choose to write about these four inventions?
   a. They are all dangerous.
   b. They are all very important.
   c. They are all unusual.
   d. They are all expensive.

In the Classroom

While completing these exercises, students should try to not look back at the reading passage to find the answers. After students have answered the questions, have them compare their answers in pairs or groups. Students should show each other where to find the answers in the passage. If your teaching situation permits, go over this exercise with students as a class. If you think students need it, create more comprehension questions based on the task type used in the chapter.

Students should record their number of correct answers in the *Reading Comprehension Chart* on page 176. Recording both their reading rate and reading comprehension score will give students an overall indication of their reading fluency.

Reading Comprehension Chart

Score	Review Reading							
	1	2	3	4	5	6	7	8
7								
6								
5								
4								
3								

Unit 1: Exam Time

Getting Ready

Answer Key

1. Answers will vary. Encourage students to share details and discuss the importance of the entrance exam system in their countries.
2. Answers will vary. Ask whether this is a good way to decide on students' futures.
3. Answers will vary. Some examples for advising the mother include telling her to help her daughter find more efficient and less stressful ways to study. Some examples for advising the daughter include having her ask other students about their preparation strategies.

Chapter 1: Oh, No, Not Another Test!

Chapter Summary

Target Vocabulary: academic, achievement, evaluate, limited, measure, memorize, proficiency, reformers

Reading Skill: Identifying Main and Supporting Ideas

Reading Passage Summary: Students take standardized tests, especially achievement and proficiency exams, but educational experts disagree about the value of these tests in making decisions about students' future directions.

Vocabulary Skill: Suffix -ize

Answer Key

Before You Read

A: 1. Answers will vary. Most students studying English will have some experience with these kinds of exams. 2. Answers will vary according to experience and language strengths and weaknesses. 3. Answers will vary according to each student's future goals.

Reading Skill

A: The main idea for paragraph 1 is that thousands of people take tests each year (lines 4–6). For paragraph 2, the main idea is that there are two main kinds of tests (line 7); and for paragraph 3, the main idea is about advocates of traditional evaluation (lines 16–18). In paragraph 4, educational reformers are the main idea (lines 21–22); and in paragraph 5, the main idea is that test experts agree that tests are not perfect (line 29).

B: 1. a is S, b is M; 2. a is S, b is M; 3. a is M, b is S; 4. a is S, b is M; 5. a is S, b is M

Reading Comprehension

A: 1. e (lines 8–10); 2. d (lines 10–12); 3. c (lines 2–6); 4. a (lines 21–35); 5. b (line 7)

B: 1. a, d (lines 8–10); 2. a, c (lines 10–13)

Critical Thinking

Answers will vary for "You." TA is test advocate, and TR is test reformer. 1. TA; 2. TR; 3. TR; 4. TA; 5. TA; 6. TR

Vocabulary Comprehension

A: 1. h; 2. e; 3. g; 4. a; 5. b; 6. c; 7. f; 8. d

B: 1. proficiency; 2. limited; 3. reform; 4. memorizing

Vocabulary Skill

A: 1. standardize; 2. memorize; 3. modernize; 4. revolutionize; 5. fantasize; 6. realize

B: 1. realize; 2. fantasize; 3. memorize; 4. revolutionize; 5. modernize; 6. standardize

C: 1. realized; 2. fantasize; 3. memorizing; 4. revolutionize

Teaching Notes

• In **Before You Read**, ask when each exam is given and whether test takers know what will be tested before taking the exam. Note that some exams listed are related to further education and others are related to finding jobs.

• After pair work, ask students whether their answers changed once they had a chance to consult with another student and why.

- In **Reading Skill**, be sure to ask students to underline main ideas and circle supporting details in pencil in case they want to make changes. Ask students to compare their answers with a partner. Remind students that supporting details give further information to support the main idea.

- The **Reading Passage** clearly defines *achievement* and *proficiency* exams, but students might benefit from a class discussion with further examples. Point out that *achievement* exams test what students have learned in a particular part of a course or program of study. Therefore, students are able to prepare for them by reviewing what they have learned. On the other hand, since *proficiency* exams assess a student's *general* level of language, you cannot directly prepare for them

other than becoming familiar with the exam tasks and formats. Everything that students do to improve their language skills contributes to their language proficiency.

- Make a distinction between exams that test *what you know* (such as facts and rules) and *what you can do*, such as performance tests where you have to actually demonstrate your skills. Discuss with students the difference between the written part of a driving test (on knowledge of traffic rules) and the practical road test.

- The **Vocabulary Skill** section notes that in British English, the suffix is spelled as *-ise*. On computers, students can adjust the spell checker to accept either British or American spelling.

Extension Activities

Writing/Reading Skill Extension: *My Worst Exam Experience*
Students write and then share about their worst exam experience.
1. Explain that everyone has had a bad exam experience. Have them brainstorm this topic.
2. Tell students that they will write one paragraph to describe their experience, so before writing, they need to consider what information is essential to include. Explain that they might want to outline the sequence of their narrative. Also explain that a "punch line" is a quick ending that suddenly explains a situation.
3. Give students 15 minutes to write and edit.
4. When students have finished writing, have each student read their paragraph to the class.
5. If time permits, ask what could be done to prevent future bad experiences.

Speaking/Listening Skill Extension: *Exam Lore: Truth or Myth?*
Students discuss ideas about standardized exams and then label each as truth or myth.
1. Ask students which standardized exams they have to take. Have students share some beliefs about the exams. For example, some students think old exams are used again, while others believe that essay topics can be predicted. Write each on the board.
2. Ask students to meet in groups of four and decide whether the ideas represent fact or fiction.
3. Have small groups then share their ideas with the rest of the class.
Note: Most standardized exams have excellent websites with reliable preparation information. After students do this activity, have them fact-check on these sites.

Integrated Skill Extension: *Exam Prep Board*
Students prepare a bulletin or notice board with exam preparation information.
1. Ask students which exams they will take in the near future. Explain that they are going to help each other be successful by sharing information and preparing together.
2. Have individuals or groups of students post the dates of important exams and what they will include (coverage of material, skills to be tested, etc.).
3. Encourage class members to develop study groups and post their meeting times and venues.
4. Note that another way to prepare is to write practice questions. Assign these as homework to be then used in the next class.

Chapter 2: For Better Grades—Use Your Brain!

Chapter Summary

Target Vocabulary: activate, components, effective, look up, make an effort, senses, technique, transfer
Reading Skill: Understanding Cause and Effect
Reading Passage Summary: By understanding how the brain works, students can learn more efficiently.
Vocabulary Skill: Word Webs

Answer Key

Before You Read

A: 1. Answers will vary. Ask students to give details to support their answers. **2.** Ask students to tell about their favorite methods for remembering important information. **3.** Have students list effective ways to study on the board.

Reading Skill

A: a. effect; **b.** cause
B: 1. b (lines 12–14); **2.** e (lines 16–18); **3.** c (lines 18–19); **4.** a (lines 21–23); **5.** d (lines 28–30)

Reading Comprehension

A: 1. three (line 9); **2.** short-term (lines 6–8, 11–12); **3.** long-term (line 16); **4.** connections (lines 17–18)
B: 1. F (lines 16–18); **2.** F (lines 34–36); **3.** T (lines 16–19); **4.** T (lines 28–30); **5.** F (lines 24–26)

Critical Thinking

1. Answers will vary. Ask who has tried some of the techniques.
2. Answers may include studying with friends, reviewing out loud, or using graphic organizers to visually order information.

Vocabulary Comprehension

A: 1. a; **2.** b; **3.** b; **4.** a; **5.** a; **6.** a; **7.** a; **8.** b
B: Answers will vary. Some possibilities: **1.** rest, recreation, fun, friends; **2.** seeing and hearing; **3.** using audio recordings; **4.** using letter associations, linking with word in your first language

Vocabulary Skill

A: *Learning* is the central idea of the word web shown, so all words should somehow connect to this theme. In the example, *memorize* is connected by a line to *remember* because memorizing is a special kind of remembering. Building on the idea of cause and effect, the word *understand* can be seen as an effect or result of learning.
B: Answers will vary. Some possibilities: **1.** *travel*: destination, type of transportation, reason to travel; **2.** *music*: type of music (rock, jazz, classical), vocal or instrumental, professional or amateur performers; **3.** *the future*: housing, lifestyle, communications, technology; **4.** *food*: categories such as fruits and vegetables, healthy vs. junk, ordinary vs. special (birthday cake, gourmet meals), natural or organic vs. processed food

Real Life Skill

A: Make sure students focus on understanding the *directions*, not answering the question. See last **Teaching Note** for suggestions.
B: 1. c (the nicest); **2.** some; **3.** a car; **4.** c

What Do You Think?

Answers will vary. Some possibilities:

1. In some countries, learning is said to be "test-driven" because tests determine what is taught in the educational system.
2. Both achievement and proficiency tests can measure progress, but students need feedback about how they are doing and how they can improve.
3. Some people would say that ability is best measured through performance tests where students actually have to use English.

Teaching Notes

- In **Before You Read**, ask what is a "good memory." What can a person with one do? Can the person remember names, numbers, past events, details from what they read? Ask whether there are any drawbacks to having a good memory. For example, someone with a photographic memory doesn't need to study very much, but maybe they can't remember information for long.
- Explain that people use different strategies for

memorizing just as people have different learning styles. For some people, color and visualization are important for memory, while others like to associate information with sounds or unrelated words.

- The **Reading Passage** describes sensory memory as having a very short duration (lines 9–10), but later it suggests that students can use sound and vision to help them learn and remember information (lines 28–32). Point out that when the senses are used actively, they can powerfully enhance memory. Ask whether students have any *scent* memories, such as associating their first school experience with the smell of chalk or new crayons.

- The **Vocabulary Skill** section introduces *word webs,* which show the connections between words. Since these connections are complex, there is no single "correct" way to construct a word web. *Word webs* are useful in a number of ways. First, some words are *superordinate* or "umbrella" terms that include many other words under them. For example, *fruit* includes apples, oranges, bananas, and berries. Often this *key word* is put in a box in the center of the word web. It is helpful for students to recognize that some words are more inclusive than

others so that they understand differences between general and more specific vocabulary items. As they gain experience with word webs, students also see that even synonyms have different shades of meaning. Another feature of word webs is that there can be many interconnections between individual words, not just one. In fact, the multiple connections resemble a spider's web, and thus the name "word *web*."

- When students develop word webs together, some will offer words that are part of their active vocabularies but which are only passively known by others in the group. Create an atmosphere where students feel comfortable asking others about words they don't know or about shades of meaning.

- In **Real Life Skills**, go over the directions for each item with the class. Ask how they are supposed to indicate their answer (circle or underline something, write it on a line, etc.). In the second item, are students only supposed to identify the incorrect item or actually change it so that it is correct? In item three, do they recognize that the pronoun "one" refers to an earlier noun? Do they identify item four as a main idea question?

Extension Activities

Listening/Speaking Skill Extension: *Memory Test*

Small groups develop and give tests of short- and long-term memory.

1. Brainstorm information associated with short- and long-term memory. For example, people store information about their families or geographic facts in their long-term memories because they learned them many years ago, but telephone numbers and new names are in short-term memory.

2. Divide the class into groups of four. Each group creates a short (five-minute) test with a mix of questions, including questions about repeating numbers or unusual names.

3. Have two groups work together and give their test to the other group. Do they notice any differences in responses according to short- and long-term memory? Encourage specific answers.

Integrated Skill Extension: *Cause and Effect Story*

Students take turns contributing lines to a narrative story.

1. Remind the class about the discourse markers that are used for cause and effect, such as *so, because, due to, therefore, consequently,* etc. Explain that each person has to add a cause and effect sentence (or two) to what the previous speakers have said. Note that as the story develops, it can get quite funny!

2. Have the first speaker start off by telling about some plans. Then have the second speaker say that things didn't work out, so something else happened. Then have the next speaker explain even more changes, and so on.

Example: **S1:** *We planned to fly to the Caribbean for our winter holiday.* **S2:** *We were late leaving home because we couldn't find our tickets.* **S3:** *We were late, so we missed our plane.* **S4:** *Due to missing our flight, we made other plans.* **S5:** *We heard there was lots of snow in the mountains. Therefore, we decided on a ski holiday instead.* **S6:** *We didn't have warm clothes because . . .*

Unit 2: Going Abroad

Getting Ready

Answer Key

1. Answers will vary, but some items—such as Disneyland—might appear in several countries (France, U.S., Hong Kong). Encourage students to be as specific as possible instead of giving answers such as "beautiful scenery" or "shopping."

2. Brainstorm about what makes a good vacation and then have students volunteer answers.

Chapter 1: Safe Travel

Chapter Summary

Target Vocabulary: sincere, assume, departure, destination, expire, local, precautions, prescriptions
Reading Skill: Scanning
Reading Passage Summary: You can have a safe and enjoyable trip by planning carefully before you depart and taking precautions while you travel.
Vocabulary Skill: Prefix *pre-*

Answer Key

Before You Read

A: 1. Answers will vary. Some possibilities for "Before your trip" include making sure documents are in order, planning for health and hygiene needs, and learning about the destination. For "During your trip," possible responses include staying in safe accommodations, being careful about food, and keeping watch on your belongings.

Reading Skill

A: 1. c

B: Before your trip: check passport, visa, and medical insurance; take medications and prescriptions; learn a little of the language. **During your trip:** prevent theft by locking hotel rooms and using the safe, use official transportation, carry a map, smile

Reading Comprehension

A: 1. T (entire reading); **2.** T (lines 6–9); **3.** F, international driver's license, *not* insurance (lines 12–13); **4.** F, doctor, *not* travel agent (lines 15–16); **5.** F, sometimes cheap hotels don't have good locks (lines 25–27).

B: 1. Look for students who might speak your language (lines 34–35). **2.** Carry medical insurance (lines 10–12). **3.** Have an international driver's license (lines 12–13). **4.** Store it in the hotel safe (lines 27–28). **5.** Use official transportation (line 30).

Critical Thinking

Answers will vary according to the culture and safety conditions in a particular country.

Vocabulary Comprehension

A: 1. b; **2.** a; **3.** a; **4.** a; **5.** b; **6.** a; **7.** b; **8.** b

B: Answers will vary. Some possibilities: **1.** a big city, a resort, a historic place, an event; **2.** Don't let mail or newspapers accumulate, let police know you'll be away. **3.** They want to learn English. **4.** foods that are specific to a country or region and not found elsewhere

Vocabulary Skill

A: 1. predict, prepared; **2.** prepaid (twice); **3.** pre-arrange; **4.** prevent; **5.** preview

B: 1. prepare; **2.** preview; **3.** predict; **4.** prevent; **5.** pre-arrange; **6.** prepaid

Teaching Notes

- In **Getting Ready**, the photographs are all of famous places in Paris: the pyramid outside the Louvre Museum, the Arc de Triomphe, and the Eiffel Tower. In the second question, some students may be more familiar with the term "holiday" than "vacation." Note that they have the same meaning.

- In **Before You Read**, emphasize that it is important to think about safe travel in the trip-planning phase as well as while you are actually traveling.

- In **Reading Skill** and **Reading Comprehension**, talk about how safe travel today requires more preparation than in the past. Explain that it is important to check the Internet for recent updates on the safety of your destination, including security issues and the political situation in that country. At many airports, travelers need extra time to check in and go through security screening. In addition, some countries have changed visa and documentation rules.

- For the **Critical Thinking** questions, have the class discuss safety issues for travelers in their city or country. In some places, you must avoid drinking tap water or eating street food. In other places, visitors must take more precautions in cities at night or when they travel on long train or bus journeys. Sometimes, women traveling alone have particular safety concerns. Ask about these.

- Several **Vocabulary Comprehension** items are particularly important for travelers. *Abroad* generally means the same thing as *overseas*. Both words imply that a *destination* is *international*, outside your own country. The opposite of departure is *arrival,* and most international airports have clearly marked areas for departing and arriving passengers. Note that airline travelers should know the words for arrival and departure in the local language.

- For the **Vocabulary Skill** in using the prefix *pre-*, point out that it means something that happens *before* something else. Encourage students to use a dictionary to find additional words that use this prefix. Ask each person to explain one new word that starts with *pre-*.

Extension Activities

Integrated Skill Extension: *Plan a Trip*
Pairs of students plan a trip and make lists to ensure that they have a safe and enjoyable trip.
1. Ask students to choose a partner with whom they will plan a trip. Have the pairs of students discuss possible destinations. Allow time for students to find information about the destinations before making a selection.
2. Tell them to write three lists: the first for things they need to do to prepare for the trip; the second for things to pack; and the third for what to do and see once they arrive at their destination.
3. Have different pairs compare their lists when they are finished. Tell each to share recommendations of additional items to include on the lists.

Example: If one group researched the weather at their destination, they were able to pack appropriate clothes. Another group may have found out about changing money upon arrival at the destination airport.

Speaking and Listening Skill Extension: *Airport Role Play*
Students brainstorm questions they are likely to be asked at an airport and then role-play travelers and officials.
1. Explain that travel often entails answering security or customs and immigration questions at an airport. Ask travelers in the class for typical questions and make note of them on the board. Some examples: *What is your destination? What are you carrying with you? Do you have any prescription medications? When does your passport expire?*
2. Ask students to work in groups of three to write a dialogue between an official and a traveler. Make sure they include the vocabulary words from this lesson.
3. Have students role-play the dialogue, taking turns being the official who asks the questions and the travelers who answer them.

Vocabulary Skill Extension: *Words with the Prefix pre-*
Students each get a word starting with the prefix *pre-*, guess its meaning, and then check.
1. Write on cards or small pieces of paper words starting with the prefix *pre-*, enough so that each student has one. Note that the words should be high-frequency words, but new words to students.
2. After writing the cards, put them in a bag or box and mix them up.
3. Have each student select a word and try to guess its meaning. Have the student look up the definition in a dictionary and compare it with the guessed meaning.
4. Have all students write the definitions on their cards, emphasizing the role of the prefix in the meaning.

Chapter 2: A Trip to Vietnam

Chapter Summary

Target Vocabulary: accommodation, amazing, exhausting, fabulous, fantastic, possessions, unique, variety
Reading Skill: Scanning for Details
Reading Passage Summary: Four e-mails describe a trip to many locations in Vietnam.
Vocabulary Skill: Adjective Endings -ed and -ing

Answer Key

Before You Read

A: Answers will vary. Some possibilities: **1. a.** Southeast Asia; **b.** hot and rainy; **c.** Hanoi (capital), Ho Chi Minh City (formerly Saigon); **d.** connections with China, France, United States; **2.** It's an interesting place and inexpensive to visit.

Reading Skill

A: 1. March 24; **2.** March 27; **3.** April 4; **4.** April 6
B: 1. Ho Chi Minh City; **2.** Cholon; **3.** three days; **4.** beaches and crafts

Reading Comprehension

A: 1. T, 3 (line 27); **2.** F, 3 (lines 24–26); **3.** F, 1 (line 3); **4.** T, 4 (lines 36–37); **5.** F, 3 (lines 19–23)
B: Cholon: 2 (lines 13–15); Ho Chi Minh City: 1 (lines 8–9); Sapa: 4 (lines 20–21); Hue: 6 (lines 19, 26–27, 30); a beach: 7 (lines 32, 34); Hanoi: 3 (line 15); a small village in the mountains: 5 (lines 21–22)

Critical Thinking

1. beautiful: amazing, colorful, took hundreds of photographs (lines 14–15)
2. friendly: kindest, friendliest, everyone smiles and says "hello" (lines 23–26)
3. comfortable: cheap, electricity, shower (lines 6, 19–20)

4. visit more of Vietnam: Three weeks here just isn't enough (line 37)

Vocabulary Comprehension

A: 1. school; **2.** terrible; **3.** relaxing; **4.** unique; **5.** plans; **6.** very bad; **7.** alike
B: 1. exhausting; **2.** accommodation; **3.** fantastic/amazing/fabulous; **4.** fantastic/amazing/fabulous; **5.** fantastic/fabulous; **6.** variety; **7.** unique

Vocabulary Skill

A: 1. excited, exciting; interested, interesting; relaxed, relaxing; confused, confusing; pleased, pleasing; stimulated, stimulating; bored, boring; worried, worrying
B: 1. interested; **2.** exciting; **3.** relaxing; **4.** stimulating; **5.** boring; **6.** worried; **7.** pleased

Real Life Skill

A: 1. c; **2.** a; **3.** e; **4.** b; **5.** f; **6.** h; **7.** g; **8.** d
B: Answers will vary according to personal information.

What Do You Think?

Answers will vary. In planning an itinerary, allow plenty of time to visit each place. Sometimes people who are familiar with a special place in their own country forget that foreign visitors may need more time to explore it. If your country is large, allow adequate time for travel from place to place.

Teaching Notes

- In **Before You Read** Part A, question 1d asks about history. Vietnam has a long and complicated history of involvement with China starting 2,200 years ago. For more than 1,000 years Vietnam was under Chinese rule, but even during periods of independence there have been times of Chinese occupation and conflict. Europeans came to Vietnam in the 16th century, and in the 19th century France established colonial rule, which lasted until 1954. At that time, the country was divided, with the United States supporting South Vietnam, resulting in a long period of warfare that ended in 1976. In recent years, Vietnam has become an economic leader in Southeast Asia and a member of the World Trade Organization.

- **Reading Comprehension** Part B asks readers to sequence the places visited. Caution students that they cannot simply scan for the place name in the e-mails and use the dates the e-mails were written. Explain that naturally, the writers are writing about places they have already visited as well as future plans for other places. Suggest that students first work out the sequence on their own, then compare their order with other students. Note that students may find it helpful to draw a time line in pencil so they can make adjustments.

- Note that the **Critical Thinking** questions are based on inference. Explain that students must find words in the Reading Passage that suggest how the writer feels about the topics. Let students spend time as a class on this task. Ask them to defend their choices with specific words from the text.
- The **Vocabulary Comprehension** section asks students to identify which of the four words doesn't fit with the others. In checking answers, ask students to be clear about how the other three words are connected. For example, in question 1, all the choices are types of buildings, but only three are businesses for overnight stays.

- Note that *fabulous* and *fantastic* are very close synonyms. Explain that both mean *amazing* or *excellent* and both words have the sense of something so good it's unreal because they come from the root word *fable* (a fairy tale) or *fantasy*. Explain that in questions 3 and 4 in Part B, *amazing, fabulous,* and *fantastic* are interchangeable and either *fabulous* or *fantastic* is possible for question 5. Note that *unique* means "one of a kind," so it is not used with the modifier "very."
- Some students confuse the adjective endings *-ed* and *-ing* presented in the **Vocabulary Skill** section. As a general rule, a *person* can be *adjective + ed* if they find *something* or *someone adjective + ing*. For example: *Peter was interested in the lecture because it was very stimulating, but Kristi was bored because she didn't find the topic interesting.*
- In **Real Life Skill**, note that ways of writing the date differ from place to place. Often forms will indicate how to write the date, for example, DD/MM/YYYY. Advise students to ask what order is expected if there is no indication on the form.

Extension Activities

Integrated Skill Extension: *Travel Agent Role Play*
Students work in pairs to plan a visit to one of the places featured in the readings.
1. Remind students that they have read about San Francisco, Vietnam, and Madrid in the unit. Have them first review the information about each place by skimming the unit.
2. Have students work in pairs, taking turns as the "travel agent" and the "tourist." Tell them to prepare a list of questions as each. For example, the tourist might ask the agent about things to do and see at various destinations, ways to travel there, and the cost of the trip. The agent might ask some of the questions from the Real Life Skill section in booking the trip. Explain that answers are not expected to be accurate, but just appropriate to the question.
3. Make sure each pair takes turns with the two roles and notes any questions that they find difficult to ask or answer.

Reading and Writing Skill Extension: *Travel Brochures*
In a follow-on to the previous activity, each student researches and makes a travel brochure.
1. Note that in doing the role play, students probably developed a curiosity about the destinations. If they have access to the Internet or print references, assign them the task of looking up information about the destination, including famous attractions or historic sites, weather, accommodations, types of transportation, etc.
2. Have students make a brochure by folding paper lengthwise. The brochures can be written content only or can contain pictures, maps, or charts of information.
3. Display the finished brochures so that students have a chance to read each other's work.

Getting Ready

Answer Key

1. The movies represent a range of *genres* or types: *Over and Over* is a drama, *Black Light* is a thriller, *Winter and Spring* is a romance, *Don't Look in the Attic* is a horror film, and *My New Job* is a comedy.

2. Responses depend on personal opinion.

Chapter 1: *Moviemaking Behind the Scenes*

Chapter Summary

Target Vocabulary: credits, director, disappear, precisely, scene, script, special effects, studio

Reading Skill: Using Titles to Understand Main Ideas

Reading Passage Summary: Although audiences are most aware of actors and directors, people who work behind the scenes are important in creating a successful movie.

Vocabulary Skill: Prefix *dis-*

Answer Key

Before You Read

A: 1. Answers will vary according to movies seen and liked; **2.** The **Reading Passage** identifies some of the key people who work behind the scenes to make movies. Some other important people are *actors* (who play parts), the *director* (who is responsible for the acting), the *producer* (who controls the film, gets funding for it, and hires actors), the *cameramen* and *sound engineers* (who record films), the *crew* (who move things around on the set), *stuntmen* (who do physically difficult moves instead of the actors), and the *editors* (who decide on what parts to leave in or to remove).

B: Students compare their answers.

Reading Skill

A: 1. just as important; **2.** look like different people; **3.** parts of the story; **4.** are not; **5.** hear

B: Students read the passage to check their answers.

Reading Comprehension

A: 1. F (lines 33–34); **2.** T (lines 28–29); **3.** F (lines 2–3); **4.** F (lines 12–14); **5.** T (lines 15–22)

B: 1. Foley artist; **2.** Special effects coordinator; **3.** Script supervisor; **4.** Makeup artist; **5.** Special effects coordinator

Critical Thinking

Answers will vary according to personal opinion.

Vocabulary Comprehension

A: 1. h; **2.** b; **3.** g; **4.** a; **5.** c; **6.** d; **7.** f; **8.** e

B: 1. Perhaps a horror film; **2.** Possibilities are *Star Wars* or *Crouching Tiger, Hidden Dragon*. **3.** See answers to question 2 in **Before You Read** Part A. **4.** Possibilities are for the departure of a train or flight, the start of a sports event or concert, a space shuttle liftoff.

Vocabulary Skill

A: 1. dishonest; **2.** disappear; **3.** disbelief; **4.** dislike; **5.** disconnected; **6.** disagree

B: 1. dislikes; **2.** disconnected; **3.** disbelief; **4.** disappear; **5.** dishonest; **6.** disagree

C: 1. dislike; **2.** dishonest; **3.** disagree; **4.** disappear

Teaching Notes

- In **Getting Ready**, students are asked to classify the movies into kinds or categories. It might be useful to activate students' background knowledge before attempting the task by asking them to brainstorm different film genres. In addition to those listed in the answer key, common types include: action, adventure, historical epic, science fiction, war or combat films, Westerns, animations, documentaries. Sometimes a very emotional film is called a "chick flick" because it primarily attracts women viewers.

- Note cultural differences in talking about *movies*, a term used most often in North America. Elsewhere, *film* or *cinema* is more common. In British English, people go to the *cinema*, not the *movies*. The word *movies* originally was a nickname for *motion pictures.*
- For more background, go to http://wikipedia.org/wiki/Filmmaking, which gives information on the overall process as well as the roles described in the **Reading Passage**.
- Another good resource for movies is the Internet Movie Database at http://imdb.com/, which provides information on current and past films as well as people in the movies.

- In **Vocabulary Skill**, *dis-* is presented as a prefix. However, some students may also know *dis* as a transitive verb made popular by hip-hop and rap musicians in the 1990s. As a verb, it means to disrespect, insult, or criticize someone and is used in informal language. For example, "Don't you dis me with that tone of voice!" means "Don't disrespect or insult me by talking that way."
- *Dislike* is a mild and polite way of saying that something does not please you. Stronger forms are *hate* and *despise*. Students should avoid the strong forms when *dislike* is what they mean.

Extension Activities

Writing/Reading Skill Extension: *My Favorite Scene*
Students write about their favorite movie scene without identifying the film, and others try to guess what it is.
1. Ask students to silently think about films they have seen and remember one scene that particularly impressed them. They will write about the scene in a single paragraph.
2. Before students start to write, caution them not to identify the name of the movie. They may mention names of characters, settings, or other details. Students write their own names on their papers.
3. After students have finished, circulate the papers so that others can read them. When readers think they know the name of the film, they should check with the writer. They should not write the name on the paper, so that others have a chance to guess.

Listening/Speaking Skill Extension: *Creating a Scene*
Small groups of students discuss what makes movie scenes memorable.
1. Students work in groups of four. Their task is to think about movie scenes that were made unforgettable by makeup or special effects.
2. Allow time for each group to discuss a variety of films before choosing one they all agree on. The group then lists the ways that makeup or special effects were used creatively.
3. Each group takes a turn describing their scene to the rest of the class. After they have described how the scene was created, allow time for other students to add information.

Integrated Skill Extension: *Name the Genre*
Students make up a review for a film and others have to guess the genre.
1. Start by reviewing the different types or genres of films that were covered earlier in the unit. It may be helpful to write these genres on the board.
2. Students work in pairs to write a brief review or movie description similar to those at the beginning of unit 3 (page 31). The reviews may be based on real films, but they should be fictional. They should exaggerate the qualities of particular genres.
3. Each pair reads their review to the rest of the class. Students try to guess what type of film it is.
Note: Sometimes a film can be a mix of several different types. For example, James Bond films combine action, adventure, mystery, and romance.

Chapter 2: Great Film Directors: Ang Lee

Chapter Summary

Target Vocabulary: academy, audience, conflict, eldest, permanently, screenplays, set in, success

Reading Skill: Recognizing Sequence of Events

Reading Passage Summary: Ang Lee has had a long and varied career in film, from his studies in film production to writing screenplay, then to directing films in both Chinese and English.

Vocabulary Skill: Organizing Vocabulary

Answer Key

Before You Read

A: 1. He's a famous director who recently won an Oscar for the film *Brokeback Mountain*. **2.** The Academy Awards or Oscars are given for the most outstanding film or achievement for each year. **3.** Other film awards are the Golden Globes and awards from major film festivals such as Cannes in France. Films are nominated for each award category, but the winner is a secret until the announcement at the actual event.

Reading Skill

A: Sequence is: 1 (studied, after he finished high school), 6 (early movies . . . in Chinese), 7 (in 1995, he moved back to the U.S., directed his first film in English), 2 (when he was 23, . . . University of Illinois), 8 (After that . . . made different kinds of movies in English), 3 (Then . . . graduate school at New York University), 9 (Academy Award . . . in 2006), 4 (After he graduated from New York University . . . wrote screenplays), 5 (In 1990, his screenplays . . .)

B: Ask students to check the sequence with the **Reading Passage**.

Reading Comprehension

A: 1. film production (lines 8–9); **2.** screenplays (line 16); **3.** Chinese, English (lines 19–25); **4.** different (line 29)

B: 1. F, a lot, not very little (lines 9–14); **2.** T (lines 22–23, 27–28); **3.** F, difficult, not easy (lines 15–16); **4.** F, in

Asia, before the United States; **5.** T (entire reading)

Critical Thinking

1. He had difficulty getting money. He wrote screenplays and won competitions.
2. There was a broader audience for English movies.

Vocabulary Comprehension

A: 1. a; **2.** b; **3.** b; **4.** a; **5.** b; **6.** b; **7.** b; **8.** a

B: 1. was set in; **2.** eldest; **3.** conflict; **4.** academy

Vocabulary Skill

A: 1. *Nouns*: director, scene, Hollywood, script, studio, credits, hero, lead actress, supervisor, monster; **2.** *Verbs*: create, avoid, disappear, produce, prepare; **3.** *Adjectives*: careful, important, impossible, famous, scary

B: 1. *People*: director, hero, lead actress, supervisor; **2.** *Places*: scene, Hollywood, studio; **3.** *Things*: script, credits, monster

C: Many combinations are possible. Here are some suggestions: **1.** a famous writer; **2.** an important event; **3.** a scary dream; **4.** a careful search; **5.** an impossible task

Real Life Skill

A: 1. b (emphasis); **2.** c (title); **3.** a (set words apart)

B: 1. scary, a; **2.** exciting, a; **3.** The Spirits, c; **4.** The Haunting of Powell Manor, c; **5.** everyone, b; **6.** invitation, a

What Do You Think?

Answers are based on personal opinions.

Teaching Notes

- From the chapter **title**, remember that a *director* is the person mainly responsible for the creative side of moviemaking. He or she must make the script come alive through what the actors and the film crew do. In addition, the director decides on the speed or pace of the development of the plot or story of the film.

- In **Before You Read**, question 3 asks about the process of award ceremonies. In general, a number of films or specific people (actors, actresses, directors, producers, etc.) are nominated. Then members of the Academy of Motion Picture Arts and Sciences (for the Oscars) or film critics vote for the best one by secret ballot. The results are made known only at the final event, which is attended by all the nominees and others in the film industry. This results in a great deal of suspense and excitement.

- The **Reading Skill** of sequencing information and events is an important, real-life skill. Information is not always presented in a neat chronological sequence. Sometimes it is jumbled or fragmentary, and the reader must use certain techniques for figuring out the sequence. If it is a biography, *key life markers* such as date of birth, childhood events, educational stages, career development, lifetime awards, retirement, and death date can be useful. Sometimes *actual dates* are given, and they can be ordered easily. Other important cues are *linking words* or discourse markers such as *ordinal numbers* (first, second), *next*, *after that*, and *finally*. Encourage students to use time lines as graphic organizers for information instead of absolutely putting events in order. Time lines allow for adjustments and later inclusion of other information, whereas just putting things in numerical order may make it difficult to adjust when new information is inserted.
- In **Vocabulary Comprehension**, the word *academy* has a range of meanings depending on context. In the sense of the *Academy of Motion Picture Arts and Sciences*, the group that gives the *Academy Awards*, it means a group or society that encourages a particular kind of activity, in this case, movies. Another example is the *French Academy*, which regulates the use of the French language. *Academy* can also refer to a particular kind of school where certain subjects, such as the arts, are emphasized. In the **Reading Passage**, Ang Lee attended an *arts academy*. In a broader sense, *academy* can refer to higher education in general, which is why university professors are referred to as *academics*.
- A *screenplay* is the written plan for a movie that includes both the action of the plot and the *dialogue* (what the actors say). Sometimes a screenplay is an adaptation of a book with more visual emphasis. At other times, it is an original script for a film. A screenplay has to include full directions for the *setting* where the film takes place and for every tiny detail of the action.
- The **Vocabulary Skill** of organizing words supports a vocabulary learning principle that the more students actually interact with words, the better they learn them.

Extension Activities

Speaking/Listening Skill Extension: *Films in My Country*
Students describe moviemaking in their own country.

1. Remind students that Hollywood is not the only place with a film industry. They may be familiar with Bollywood—the informal name of the Hindi-language film industry based in Mumbai, India—or with other places that are known for film production. Ask what is happening with films in their own country. Sometimes, even if there is not a developed moviemaking industry, the country is used as a location for films.
2. After students have responded in general, ask whether there is a particular type of film made locally. What kinds of films are popular? Are foreign films subtitled in the local language?

Integrated Skill Extension: *Jigsaw Sequencing*
Pairs of students produce a jigsaw challenge and give it to another pair to solve.

1. Explain that pairs of students will write a sequence of six steps. The steps can be from a person's life (as in the lesson), from a narrative that tells a story, from recounting a sports or news event, or even from a folk tale. The important thing is that there must be some sort of clue for each step and students must use connectors to link the steps.
2. As the students develop their sequence, they can use scratch paper. However, when they have finalized their sequence, each of the six steps should be on separate, unnumbered pieces of paper. These papers should then be randomly jumbled so they are not in any fixed order.
3. Pairs of students give their jumbled sequence to another set of students. The puzzle-solvers read the individual steps and then discuss out loud the options for putting them into sequence. As they do so, they should physically move the pieces of paper around on a desk or table.
4. When the first pair has solved the sequence, they give their scrambled sequence to the other team to solve. Groups can mingle and solve sequences as long as time permits.

Unit 4: Sports Heroes

Getting Ready

Answer Key
A: Answers will vary. There are hundreds of sports that could be included.

B: Some of the more common team sports are football, basketball, baseball, soccer, volleyball, and hockey. Individual sports include cycling, gymnastics, skiing, skating, auto racing, diving, and weightlifting. Most of these sports are Olympic events with the exceptions of cycling and auto racing.

Chapter 1: Sports History

Chapter Summary

Target Vocabulary: enthusiastic, establish, extend, league, professional, regulation, season, supporters
Reading Skill: Scanning
Reading Passage Summary: Although baseball, golf, and skiing are now international sports, each has an interesting history in particular countries.
Vocabulary Skill: Using *Play* and *Go* with Sports and Games

Answer Key

Before You Read
A: 1. the United States; **2.** Scotland; **3.** 1700s;
   4. Norwegians; **5.** transportation

Reading Skill
A: 1. baseball; **2.** golf; **3.** skiing

Reading Comprehension
A: 1. North America (the north), Latin America (lines 4–5);
   2. Edinburgh (lines 17–18); **3.** St. Andrews Links (lines 21–22); **4.** ski lifts (lines 37–39)
B: 1. golf (line 15) and skiing (line 36); **2.** skiing (lines 31–35); **3.** baseball (lines 5–7); **4.** golf (lines 17–18);
   5. all three sports (entire reading)

Critical Thinking
1. Answers will vary depending on where the student lives and media exposure.

2. Possible answers are through the movement of people (migration) and trends.
3. Answers will vary.

Vocabulary Comprehension
A: 1. reduce; **2.** amateur; **3.** independent; **4.** opinion;
   5. close; **6.** uninterested; **7.** critic; **8.** variety
B: 1. supporter, season; **2.** extends; **3.** regulations;
   4. league, established

Vocabulary Skill
A: Go: skiing, jogging, swimming, cycling, surfing, skateboarding; **Play:** soccer, golf, tennis, chess, baseball, basketball
B: 1. play; **2.** playing, playing; **3.** go, play; **4.** playing;
   5. go; **6.** go; **7.** play

Teaching Notes

- For more information about sports in the **Getting Ready** section, consult Wikipedia at http://en.wikipedia.org/sports. See http://olympic.org for official Olympic sports. For part B, have students work in pairs to mark sports as team, individual, or Olympic, and then have them check their answers as homework. Be sure to keep the resulting list of sports for one of the **Extension Activities** below.
- The **Reading Passage** is full of details, so select some to give students additional practice in scanning for specific information. After they have looked for a number of

  items, ask them to quickly re-read the passage with a different emphasis, to get the general meaning or gist of each paragraph. Explain that this is called *skimming*. To make the point, ask students to skim one paragraph at a time and then close their books. Ask general questions about the paragraph before proceeding.
- Answers to the **Critical Thinking** questions will depend on the students' background knowledge. For question 2, ask about the ways ideas can spread. In the past,

it was by people physically moving from place to place (cricket spread with British colonialism). Now, international media such as television and the Internet spread information about sports without anyone leaving home. Ask what unusual sports students have seen on television to emphasize the last point. Have they ever seen skeleton races, curling, bocce, or lacrosse? Make note of the sports students mention.

- Have students do **Vocabulary Comprehension** part A by themselves before checking answers with a partner. To build vocabulary, pairs of students should discuss their reasons for grouping some words together and eliminating other words. For example, in item 2 *amateur* and *professional* are clearly opposites, but either could be *skilled* or *expert* in a particular sport. Ask about why an athlete is considered an amateur or a professional.

- In the **Vocabulary Skill** section, note that *go* is used with sports ending with an *-ing* suffix as well as other activities such as shopping. *Play* is used with sports and activities with a variety of endings and can be extended to play piano and other musical instruments.

Extension Activities

Integrated Skill Extension: *Rules and Regulations*
Students work in small groups to define the regulations for well-known sports.
1. Brainstorm well-known sports. Write the names on the board. Point out that the students probably know the regulations for these sports very well, but people in other countries may not.
2. Explain that the class will take some foreign visitors to local sports events, and they need to prepare the visitors by giving them an overview of the rules and regulations. Provide some questions for the students to think about: Who can score and under what conditions? When do teams take turns? When is someone out of the game? What moves are allowable and which are illegal?
3. Ask students to work in groups of four with each group selecting a different sport. Have the groups discuss the basic regulations for their sport and write them on a chart.
4. Have each group present its set of regulations to the rest of the class, who give them feedback.

Speaking/Listening Skill Extension: *Team Scream*
As sports are called out, teams of students make decisions about the sport and shout answers.
1. Go back to the long list of sports the students generated during **Getting Ready**. Divide the class into team 1, team 2, and team 3. Explain that you will call out a sport from the list and the designated team has to answer several questions: Is the verb *go* or *play* used with this sport? Is it a team or individual sport? Is it an Olympic sport? Explain that teams can discuss together before answering questions and that each question is one point.
2. Start the quiz with team 1. Let the other teams know that if team 1 can't answer all three questions, then team 2 gets a chance to answer, and so on. Explain that when a team gets all three answers, they get another sport again, but when they make a mistake, the next team gets a chance to play.
3. Continue until all sports names have been used and then tally scores.
Note: You will need a scorekeeper for this game.

Integrated Skill Extension: *Unusual Sports Challenge*
Students research unusual sports, then challenge their classmates about the sport.
1. As a follow-on to **Critical Thinking** question 3, assign students the task of researching an unusual sport for homework. By using "unusual sports" as the search term on the Internet, they can find many little-known sports such as pelota, bozkashi, or roque.
2. Explain that basic information required is: a) the name of the sport; b) where it is played; and c) a brief description of what type of sport it is. For example: *Bozhashi is played in Afghanistan by teams of horseback riders who try to capture a goat and take it across a goal line.* Let students note that any photos of the sport or its equipment would be very helpful.
3. In class, have students write the name of their sport on the board. Let other students try to share any information they know about the sport. Then, have the student who did the research correct any wrong points and give any additional information.

Chapter 2: *Sports Success: Yao Ming*

Chapter Summary

Target Vocabulary: adjust, championship, coach, enroll, extremely, sense of humor, record, youth
Reading Skill: Predicting
Reading Passage Summary: Yao Ming, a very tall basketball player whose talents were recognized in his native China, now plays for the Houston Rockets in the United States.
Vocabulary Skill: Adjectives with the Suffix *-ous*

Answer Key

Before You Read

1. Answers will vary according to countries and opinions.
2. Possible answers are strength, agility or ability to move well, good coordination, and a quick mind.
3. Students can see that he is a tall basketball player of Chinese background, playing with non-Chinese players.

Reading Skill

A: On the basis of the photo, students are likely to choose physical strength and the right body type.
B: After reading the article, students may add information about coaches, personality, and family.

Reading Comprehension

A: 1. athletes (lines 6–8); **2.** a teenager (lines 10–14); **3.** Houston (lines 2–3, 25, 36); **4.** commercials (lines 31–32); **5.** funny (line 30)
B: 1. F, *wasn't* interested (lines 7–10); **2.** F, because he was *tall* (lines 8–13); **3.** T (lines 14–18); **4.** F, *wasn't* very happy (lines 25–27); **5.** T (lines 27–37)

Critical Thinking

1. Yao's first year probably had many adjustments to living in the United States that would be interesting to the public.
2. Differences between Chinese and American cultures, the support of his coaches and family

Vocabulary Comprehension

A: 1. a; **2.** b; **3.** a; **4.** b; **5.** a; **6.** b; **7.** b; **8.** a
B: 1. championship; **2.** record; **3.** coach; **4.** extremely;

5. adjusted; **6.** youth; **7.** enrolled

Vocabulary Skill

A: humorous; dangerous; famous; courageous; nervous; adventurous
B: 1. famous; **2.** nervous; **3.** dangerous; **4.** courageous; **5.** humorous; **6.** adventurous
C: 1. and **2.** Any of the words fit here. **3.** humorous; **4.** dangerous; **5.** Any of the words fit here. **6.** dangerous, courageous, humorous, or adventurous

Real Life Skill

A: Answers will vary. Note that some countries use a variety of forms depending on the document.
B: Make sure students use ordinal forms for days, i.e., February seventeenth, two thousand seven; **C: 1.** March 4, 2007; **2.** 3 May 2002; **3.** 1 December 1999; **4.** July 12, 2005; **5.** 8 September 2008; **6.** April 2, 2006

What Do You Think?

Answers will vary according to experience and opinion. Some suggestions:

1. Students who actively play sports may enjoy playing some and watching others. Students who don't play sports may like watching some sports but not all.
2. Some educators believe that requiring participation in school sports establishes a lifelong habit of exercise, which is good for health. Others believe playing team sports helps students learn to work well in a group and learn teamwork skills for life.
3. Some sports heroes, such as Lance Armstrong, have overcome health or other problems to compete successfully in their sport.

Teaching Notes

- Note that the chapter **Title** uses *sports* in the plural as is common in American English. In British English, *sport* in the singular is more common, as in the BBC television program *World Sport*.

- In **Reading Skill**, students may base their predictions on what they can see in the picture, not invisible factors such as a supportive family and the right personality. After reading the article, they may be far more likely to include factors such as hard work and good coaching.

- Encourage students to build the habit of predicting before they start to read. Before any reading, have them pay attention to pictures, captions, titles, and headlines, then make very brief notes on what they expect that the reading will cover. Prediction activates students' background knowledge about a topic, and it also provides a framework into which they can fit new information from the reading. Students must pay careful attention to the source and date of the reading, the author's purpose, and the type of reading text. For example, students who are used to reading about sports personalities in popular magazines might be surprised to read a more objective encyclopedia account of the athlete's career.

- Note that the biographical **Reading Passage** provides a natural opportunity to recycle other reading skills such as sequencing information through the use of a time line. Ask students to put the main events of Yao's life on a time line running from his birth to the present. Have them select the most important events and sequence them.

- In **Vocabulary Skill**, note that in many cases the addition of the suffix -*ous* to a noun ending in "e" means that the letter is omitted. However, there are some exceptions, such as *courageous*.

- **Real Life Skill** presents alternative ways of expressing dates. There is a movement toward an international standard of giving the date followed by the month and year, so even in the United States there are government forms with a DDMMYYYY format. Caution students to take particular care when filling out forms online since they are sometimes unclear about the order intended.

Extension Activities

Speaking/Listening Skill Extension: Debate: *Athletes Are Born, Not Made*

Students form two teams to debate the premise that athletes owe their success to innate factors such as size and strength instead of to training and coaching.

1. Explain the premise to be debated and allow some general discussion before choosing teams. You might want to include current issues such as the use of steroids to enhance performance.
2. Allow students who feel strongly about one side of the issue to volunteer for that team. Assign the other students to the second team. Make sure the class is divided evenly into two teams.
3. Allow time for the teams to organize their positions and statements.
4. Give each team an opportunity to present their position and for a rebuttal.

Integrated Skill Extension: *Sports Editors I*

Use sports pages from newspapers to select headlines and short articles as well as photographs and captions for students to sort into sports pages.

1. Note that this activity requires some preparation, which can be done by the teacher or by the class. Assign each student one sports article, including headlines, to cut out and bring to class, or one sports photograph with a caption. Before the activity, scramble all the newspaper cutouts.
2. Give each student two newspaper cutouts. Tell them they must predict what the matching piece will look like. Have each student make brief notes about their predictions.
3. Let students then circulate to find the missing parts. Have students place the matches on a central table or desk.
4. When all matches are made, ask what kinds of information were most useful in finding the matching parts. For example, were sports uniforms especially useful in finding teams?

Reading and Writing Skill Extension: *Sports Editors II*

Students identify sports vocabulary from newspaper sports articles as a follow-on from the previous skill extension or a free-standing activity.

1. Have individual students read sports pages to find five words or phrases that are new to them. They try to figure out the meaning of the words according to the context of the article.
2. Tell students to write the new vocabulary items on separate pieces of paper along with the sentence or context in which they were found. Have them also write the meaning that they guess and then post the vocabulary on a board or put it on a flat surface for other students to read and add their interpretations.
3. Talk about sports idioms or particular collocations after everyone looks at the vocabulary, and add their comments.

Getting Ready

Answer Key

1. Clockwise from top right: brain, heart, lung, stomach, intestine, bone, joint, skin, muscle

2. The *brain* controls the functions of the rest of the body. The *heart* pumps blood through the body. The *lungs* exchange carbon dioxide for oxygen. The *stomach* and *intestine* help the body digest food and get rid of waste. The *bones* and *skeleton* provide the framework for the body. *Joints* enable limbs (arms and legs) to move. The *skin* protects the rest of the body. *Muscles* contract and relax so that the body can move.

3. Some other body parts include the *kidneys* (get rid of waste), *spleen* (produces blood cells), *liver* (filters blood and changes sugar to glucose), and *pancreas* (aids digestion).

Chapter 1: You Are Amazing: You Are Human!

Chapter Summary

Target Vocabulary: breathe, clinic, complex, digest, illness, poisoning, suffer, treatment

Reading Skill: Skimming for the Main Idea

Reading Passage Summary: The human body is an amazingly complex machine that requires care and attention to function well for a lifetime.

Vocabulary Skill: Root Words Related to Life; Nouns Ending in *-logy/-ology*

Answer Key

Before You Read

A: 1. Answers will vary. Note that visitors and patients see hospitals from different perspectives.
2. Possibilities include a disease, injuries from an accident, or even childbirth. 3. Answers may range from diagnostic exams to surgery.

Reading Skill

A: 1. 3

B: The first answer choice is "a," and the second is "b." By paragraph numbers: 1. a; 2. a; 3. b; 4. a; 5. b

Reading Comprehension

A: 1. unaware (lines 8–10); 2. smoking, drinking alcohol, eating junk food (lines 11–13); 3. injury and poisoning (lines 17–18); 4. gerontology, the population of elderly people has increased (lines 25–26)

B: 1. very little (lines 8–10); 2. accidents (lines 17–18); 3. has many complicated parts (lines 5–8); 4. old people (lines 22–23)

Critical Thinking

Answers will vary. Some suggestions: 1. Some parts cannot be replaced, bad habits have an effect. 2. Exercise, eat healthy food, get enough rest, and smile often.

Vocabulary Comprehension

A: 1. b; 2. b; 3. a; 4. b; 5. a; 6. b; 7. a; 8. b

B: Answers will vary. 1. A serious illness requires medical care and does not go away by itself. 2. exercise, running, being scared; 3. Spicy or greasy food is difficult to digest, but plain food like rice is easy to digest. 4. Avoid food for a day or two, drink clear liquids.

Vocabulary Skill

A: bio, life; psych, mind; phon, sound; physio, nature/body; geo, earth

B: 1. biology; 2. psychology; 3. geology; 4. phonology; 5. physiology

C: 1. biology; 2. physiology; 3. phonology

Teaching Notes

- There are a number of websites for study of the human body. See http://www.innerbody.com/htm/body.html to learn about systems of the body and how they work. BBC's Human Body and Mind site at http://www.bbc. co.uk/science/humanbody/ has interactive games and many interesting articles. Use "human body" as the search term to find more information.

- In **Before You Read**, remember that hospital care

varies depending on location and culture. In some places, going to the hospital is a fairly ordinary event, but in other places it happens only in dire or life threatening situations. If the latter is the case for your students, be sensitive to their concerns about discussing hospitalization.

- Before students do the **Reading Skill** section, review the differences between main ideas and supporting details. Remind students that a main idea usually appears in the topic sentence of a paragraph and is followed by examples or further details. Consider using an outline or graphic organizer to go through the parts of the reading. For example, the graphic organizer called a *spider map* has the topic in the center (in this case, the human body) with main idea lines radiating out in all directions (on which you would write the main idea for each paragraph), with supporting details radiating from those. Note that

demonstrating how this works with the **Reading Passage** content will also give students a useful tool to use on their own with other readings.

- Remind students that while both *skimming* and *scanning* involve reading quickly, they entail reading for different levels of information. Sometimes a visual image helps to remind them of the difference. If you are in a fast boat *skimming* over the water, you only have time to look for large things such as big rocks. However, if you put a page from a book in a *scanner*, it's going to copy every detail.

- Note that *physiology* is one of the examples in the **Vocabulary Skill** section on the suffix *-ology*. Point out that while anatomy is the study of the systems of the body (circulatory, digestive, reproductive, etc.), physiology is concerned with the processes of the body, how the body functions.

Extension Activities

Vocabulary Skill Extension: *Health Word Sort*
Students brainstorm health-related words and sort them into categories.
1. Ask students for any words they can think of that are related to the human body, health, or medicine. As words are suggested, quickly write them on the board in any order. Elicit as many words from the class as you can.
2. Brainstorm four or five major categories for the words. Some suggestions that use recent vocabulary include *human body* (many words from this unit), *problems* (illness, injury, poisoning), *medical care* (treatment, prescription), and *places* (hospital, clinic, doctor's office).
3. Divide the class into as many groups as you have categories. Explain that each group is responsible for going through the entire list and deciding which words belong in their category. Note that groups should also add other words as they think of them. Point out that some words may fit into more than one category.
4. Ask each group to present their list to the class for comments or additions.

Speaking/Listening Skill Extension: *Doctor/Patient Role Play*
Following the vocabulary activation exercise, students work in pairs to role-play doctors and patients.
1. Explain that everyone will take turns being the doctor or the patient, so everyone needs to think of typical dialogues in a doctor's office. Ask for words describing typical *symptoms* such as *pain, fever, cough,* or *rash*. What kinds of questions is a doctor likely to ask? Elicit words for different types of treatments (*give a prescription, get an X-ray, take aspirin, rest quietly,* etc.). Remind the class about the forms of giving advice (*I think you should . . . You ought to . . . You must . . .*).
2. When most of the class seems comfortable with the vocabulary and structures, ask students to work in pairs. Have them take turns as doctor and patient with the following steps: a) the "patient" says what's wrong; b) the "doctor" asks for information and the patient responds; and c) the "doctor" gives advice. Sometimes, the "doctor" can show cause and effect: *"You fell on your arm, so now it's broken."* Make sure students switch roles.
3. Ask some pairs of students to volunteer to do their role play for the rest of the class.
4. Allow time at the end for students to ask questions about additional useful vocabulary or procedure.
Note: This activity is intended to provide practice for students in real-life situations.

Chapter 2: Beyond the Body's Limits

Chapter Summary

Target Vocabulary: cope, demonstrate, determination, endurance, recover, resilient, severe, strain
Reading Skill: Predicting Vocabulary
Reading Passage Summary: British rower Steve Redgrave overcame two severe illnesses through determination and training to win a gold medal at the Olympics in 2000.
Vocabulary Skill: Suffix -tion

Answer Key

Before You Read

A: 1. The sport is rowing, done in special small boats with one or several people rowing. **2.** Olympic athletes have to be the most outstanding in their sport for their country. They have to have great strength, endurance, and determination to win.

Reading Skill

A: Answers will vary.
B: Actual words in the reading are *team, athlete, strain, medal, training, strength, endurance, stress, determination,* and *body.*

Reading Comprehension

A: 1. F, from Britain, not Sydney (lines 1–2); **2.** F, after, not before (lines 9–14); **3.** T (lines 11–13); **4.** T (lines 23–24); **5.** F, weak, not very strong (lines 29–30)
B: 1. appendicitis, diabetes (lines 11–14); **2.** giving up, decided to continue (lines 17–20); **3.** put stress on their bodies, use courage and determination to overcome limits (lines 25–34); **4.** and his team won a gold medal (lines 34–35)

Critical Thinking

1. The author admires him.
2. Resilient, courage, determination, overcome, amazing, achievement

Vocabulary Comprehension

A: 1. e; **2.** c; **3.** h; **4.** f; **5.** g; **6.** d; **7.** b; **8.** a
B: 1. endurance; **2.** determination; **3.** Recovering; **4.** strain; **5.** resilient; **6.** demonstrate; **7.** severe; **8.** cope

Vocabulary Skill

A: 1. determination; **2.** demonstration; **3.** injection; **4.** competition; **5.** participation
B: For items **1** and **2**, either *participate* or *compete* can be used. **3.** demonstrate; **4.** determination; **5.** competition; **6.** injection; **7.** participation

Real Life Skill

A: Students should note there are two forms referring to eye and foot.
B: 1. c; **2.** e; **3.** f; **4.** b; **5.** d; **6.** a
C: 1. 555-2356; **2.** 555-8855; **3.** 555-2234; **4.** 555-0076; **5.** 555-6789; **6.** 555-9080

What Do You Think?

Answers will vary. Some suggestions:
1. Rest, see a doctor, take medications.
2. Exercise more, eat a healthier diet.
3. Lance Armstrong, who won the Tour de France despite cancer; Eric Weihenmayer, a blind man who climbed Mount Everest

Teaching Notes

- **Before You Read** asks about *rowing*, a competitive sport in which racers row in small boats called *sculls*. Both men and women row, individually or in teams in a boat. When there are teams, the leader, called a *coxswain* or *cox*, gives orders or directions to the rowers. In American universities the popular sport is called *crew*. Rowing requires both strength and endurance.

- The **Reading Skill** of vocabulary prediction activates background knowledge, including passive vocabulary that the reader may recall in the context of the reading. It also aids the process of word association by tying what the reader already knows to new vocabulary items.

- The **Reading Passage** is largely about the achievements of Steve Redgrave despite severe health problems. Redgrave won a gold medal in rowing five times in a row (from 1984 to 2000) and has won more championships than any other rower in the world. For his achievements he has won numerous awards, including being knighted in 2001—so he is actually Sir Stephen Redgrave. In addition to his successes in rowing, Redgrave participates competitively in other sports. In 1989–90 he was a member of the British bobsled team, and he also ran and finished in the London Marathon. See http://en.wikipedia.org/wiki/Stephen_Redgrave for more information.

- The **Critical Thinking** task uses vocabulary as a way of making inferences about the writer's opinion. Point out to students that some words are not neutral; they have positive or negative values and are used to indirectly give opinions. The words here are all very complimentary about Redgrave's personal qualities and his achievements.

- Provide more practice with the **Real Life Skill** by bringing in telephone book listings of physicians or downloading lists from hospital sites on the Internet. Ask students to work in pairs to figure out what the specialties are.

Extension Activities

 Speaking/Listening Skill Extension: *Who Am I?*
Sticky labels with names of famous athletes are put on students' backs, and they have to figure out who they are.

1. Brainstorm a list of famous athletes and then distribute one blank label to each person. Have each student write an athlete's name on the label and return the labels to a central place where they are scrambled. Make sure there are enough self-stick labels for everyone in the class.
2. Demonstrate the process. Start by asking for a volunteer. Place a label on the student's back without the student seeing what is written. Then have the student go around the class asking yes/no questions about who s/he is. Explain that other students can read what is written, but under no circumstances can they give away the name. For example, if the name is Lance Armstrong, the student could ask, *"Am I a female athlete? Am I a famous skier? Do I play on a team? Did I win a gold medal in the Olympics?"* and so on until the identity is guessed.
3. When everyone understands how to play, have the first volunteer put labels on the backs of the rest of the class, taking care that they do not see what is written.
4. When identities have been guessed, ask the class which questions were most helpful.

 Reading/Vocabulary Skill Extension: *Writer's Opinion*
Students read about famous athletes and use inference to decide the author's opinion based on vocabulary.

1. Have students read an article by a sports writer about a well-known athlete. Note that the article can be from a newspaper, a sports magazine, or the Internet.
2. Explain that the first reading is skimming for comprehension of the gist. Have students note whether the writer feels positively or negatively about the athlete.
3. Explain that the second reading is a close reading with attention to vocabulary. Have students identify words that support the author's opinion, and make note of the words.
4. Note that it may be more convenient for students to do this exercise as homework. If that is the case, give time to go over the words in class in order to create more awareness of words used in opinions.

 Listening Skill Extension: *Speaker's Opinion*
Students listen to a sports broadcast and identify words that express opinion.

1. Note that listening may prove a bit more challenging, but it is a Real Life Skill since many sports fans regularly listen to radio or television sports broadcasts. Explain that it does not matter whether words are spelled correctly since the goal is critical listening.
2. Note that another variant is listening to sports commentators talk about teams they like and don't like, which is particularly easy to do during the playoff season leading up to championship games or matches.

Unit 6: Leisure and Hobbies

Getting Ready

Answer Key
A: 1. sleep; **2.** work; **3.** leisure; **4.** household; **5.** other

B: Answers will vary.

Chapter 1: Scrapbooking

Chapter Summary

Target Vocabulary: decorate, define, display, precious, preserve, supplies, throw away, universal
Reading Skill: Finding Definitions
Reading Passage Summary: Scrapbooking is a popular new hobby in which people combine photographs, writing, and decorations to preserve important family events and memories.
Vocabulary Skill: Suffix -ment

Answer Key

Before You Read

A: Answers will vary. Some suggestions: **1.** People often keep photos in albums or in storage boxes, but increasingly, digital photos are stored on computers; **2.** Travel mementos or souvenirs include tickets, programs, menus, matchbook covers, maps, or brochures; **3.** In addition to photos, parents often save report cards, drawings, or even the first tooth their child lost.

Reading Skill

A: An empty book for collecting and preserving photographs, newspaper articles, and other papers. The word *scrapbook* was in italics, and the definition was surrounded by quotes.

B: layout: a page with fancy paper, stickers, drawings, and words about a theme; **scrappers:** people who make scrapbooks; **crops:** parties where people work on scrapbooks and share information about them

Reading Comprehension

A: 1. save bits of paper and look at them to remember (lines 16–17); **2.** her father died (lines 17–18); **3.** her father (lines 17–21); **4.** preserve family history, display it (line 29)

B: 1. T (lines 31–33); **2.** T (lines 32–34); **3.** F, party, not competition (lines 24–26); **4.** F, personal or family history, not national history (lines 14, 26, 29–31, 35);

5. T (lines 3–4, 8–9)

Critical Thinking

1. Stereotypes might indicate old and female, but actually many young people and men are interested in the hobby.
2. Negative responses include expense and reminders of unpleasant parts of the past.
3. Answers will vary, but probably family life or important events.

Vocabulary Comprehension

A: 1. f; **2.** a; **3.** e; **4.** c; **5.** d; **6.** h; **7.** g; **8.** b

B: 1. Photos, stories, special belongings; **2.** Something that is no longer important to your life; **3.** Answers will vary, but pictures and posters are often used. **4.** Eating meals with others, sports, family celebrations such as weddings

Vocabulary Skill

A: 1. achievement, succeeding in doing something; **2.** measurement, finding the size of something; **3.** development, making something better or bigger; **4.** requirement, something that is needed or must be done; **5.** agreement, an arrangement or promise by two or more people; **6.** government, the people who rule or govern a country or place

B: 1. achievement; **2.** agree; **3.** requirement; **4.** improve; **5.** improvement; **6.** measurement

C: Answers will vary but should include one noun each.

Teaching Notes

- *Leisure*, the **Unit Topic**, means free time away from work or tasks such as homework. It is a time for people to rest, play sports, or have fun with their hobbies. Social scientists point out that leisure is a product of the Industrial Revolution, when workers first had time off. Leisure is pronounced differently in American and British English. In

British English, it rhymes with "pleasure."

- In **Getting Ready** and again in **Chapter 2**, students are asked to read charts and graphs. The *pie chart* in Getting Ready is a visual way to show the relative sizes of parts of a whole. In this case, it shows the proportion of hours that people spend doing certain activities in a day. Remind students that the individual sections must add up to 24 hours for a day. Six hours would be 25% or a quarter slice of the pie chart.

- For years people have kept photos in albums, but *scrapbooking* goes far beyond simple photo albums. As described in the **Reading Passage**, people combine many materials to create an elaborate finished product that is intended to be saved by the family. Scrapbookers use fancy papers, photographs, and *decorations* that are called *embellishments*. These include stickers, stamps, ribbons, and other mementos. Many of the items are cut into special shapes with scissors or die cut machines. *Journaling*—a written description or a story—is an important part of scrapbooking because it tells the reader about the people and events in the scrapbook.

- With the development of digital photography and desktop publishing, digital scrapbooks have become popular for several reasons. First, original photographs and memorabilia are not damaged in the process because they have been scanned and saved. Second, digital scrapbooks can be shared with others online, and they can also be stored electronically. In addition, if you have a computer, digital scrapbooks are less expensive because many components are available free.

- The **Reading Skill** notes that definitions are often indicated by quotation marks, parentheses, or dashes, but there are other ways to indicate a definition or synonym. *Apposition* is when two nouns or noun phrases follow each other, the second being set off with commas. For example, *"The coxswain, the leader of the rowing team, sits in a forward position"* defines the word *coxswain*. Other common ways of providing definitions within the text include the conjunction "or" and using special formatting such as *italics* or **bold**.

- In **Vocabulary Comprehension**, the word *precious* can have a literal meaning of something that is very expensive or valuable (*a precious gem like a diamond*) or a figurative meaning of much loved or very important (*her precious little granddaughter*). *Preserve* can be a *verb*—to save something—or a *noun*—something that is saved, such as a *nature preserve* or a jar of *fruit preserves*.

Extension Activities

Integrated Skill Extension: *Charting My Weekend*
Students track how they spend time during a weekend and put the information on a pie chart.
1. Identify a 48-hour period as the weekend. For example, from Friday at 7 p.m. to Sunday at 7 p.m.
2. Explain that each student will keep a log of what they do in this 48-hour period. Have them make detailed entries such as "played tennis 9:15–10:45 a.m.," or "went shopping at Mega Mall for new shoes." Make sure they also log "down time" or time spent just relaxing and doing nothing in particular.
3. Note that although students could use the categories from page 69, it would be better if they made their own. Some possibilities are personal care (haircut, shower), socializing (time with friends), or communications (time on mobile phone or sending e-mails). Categories will differ.
4. At the end of the weekend, have students tally up the hours spent in each category. Have them divide those hours by 48 to get a percentage that determines the size of the "slice" in the pie chart.
5. Explain that the next step is writing a brief reflective paragraph on the way time was spent. Does the log fit their previous idea of how they spend their time? Would they do things differently? How?
6. In class, have students meet in groups of four to compare their charts and discuss them.

Writing Skill Extension: *Plan a Scrapbook*
Students plan a small scrapbook about an important life or family event.
1. Have the class brainstorm about events for which they would like to do a scrapbook, such as family weddings, graduation, a sports championship, or a class trip.
2. Remind the class that effective scrapbooks contain a mix of photos, writing, and decorations.
3. Have each person select an event and make planning notes about what to include in the scrapbook. What kinds of things should be saved as mementos? What would be good photos to take?

Chapter 2: Work Hard, Play Hard?

Chapter Summary

Target Vocabulary: chores, commuting, conduct, hectic, pursue, pursuits, ranked, well-being
Reading Skill: Identifying Main Ideas within Paragraphs
Reading Passage Summary: Having time to pursue leisure activities is important for everyone, but surveys show that favorite activities vary enormously from country to country and over time.
Vocabulary Skill: Word Associations

Answer Key

Before You Read
A: 1–4. Answers will vary according to individual lifestyles. See the **Teaching Notes** for suggestions.

Reading Skill
A: 1. b
B: By paragraph numbers: **2.** a; **3.** a; **4.** a; **5.** b

Reading Comprehension
A: 1. the U.K. (lines 15–17); **2.** Japan (lines 17–19); **3.** the U.S. (lines 13–15)
B: 1. traveling to and from work (lines 3–4); **2.** relax (lines 8–9); **3.** different (lines 12–21); **4.** increasing (lines 29–31); **5.** more (lines 34–36)

Critical Thinking
1. To emphasize that people have limited time for leisure;
2. Answers will vary with country.

Vocabulary Comprehension
A: 1. hectic; **2.** staying in one place; **3.** hobby; **4.** stop; **5.** mix up; **6.** chore; **7.** stress; **8.** follow
B: 1. chore; **2.** commuting, hectic; **3.** pursue; **4.** pursuits

Vocabulary Skill
A: Remind the class about general and specific words. A hobby is a type of activity. The relationship between scissors and paper is quite different. Scissors are a tool you use to cut paper.

B: 1. hobby; **2.** download, e-mail; **3.** commuting; **4.** enjoy; **5.** hectic; **6.** common
C: Many associations are possible, but here are some suggestions: **1.** relax, fun, enjoy, weekend, leisure, holiday; **2.** travel, vacation, fly, train, bus, tickets, reservation, hotel, destination; **3.** school, class, student, teacher, books, homework, exams

Real Life Skill
A: Some other possibilities are rock, jazz, hit tunes, pop stars.
B: 1. digital photos, electronic camera; **2.** tropical fish, saltwater fish tank; **3.** easy recipes, learn to cook; **4.** famous film stars, Hollywood actors, movie stars, celebrities
C: Answers will vary depending on search engines.

What Do You Think?
Answers will vary. Some suggestions:
1. Some people like to relax by exercising. Other people like some quiet time alone.
2. In countries where people work long hours or commute for long distances, they have very little time to relax or pursue hobbies during the workweek.
3. Internet activities, computer games, and certain sports (skateboarding) are very popular with young people in many countries. Some older people prefer tai chi, needlework, or bird-watching.

Teaching Notes

- The **Before You Read** section features surveys, as does the **Reading Passage**. Ask students whether they have ever participated in a survey, either by interview or by filling out a questionnaire. Ask why people conduct surveys. Possible answers are to get information about marketing products or entertainment such as films and TV programs. The survey in **Before You Read** shows three of the most familiar types of survey questions: agreement with or description of a statement, information in categories, or a scale where items are ranked from best to worst.

- Before attempting **Before You Read** Part A, item 2, ask students about *commuting*, traveling regularly between two places. This could be home and school or work. Ask how students commute to classes.

- You can follow up on item 4 in the survey by asking how many students marked each category as "1," the favorite activity. Put the numbers on the board and ask the class to make statements about the ranking of popular activities.

- The **Reading Passage** refers to leisure, free time, and spare-time activities as being the same. However, note that no sports are mentioned, nor are many hobbies. Some people distinguish between leisure as a general concept and recreation as a more specific and active form that includes participation in sports and going on holidays. The contrast doesn't hold fast because in the United Kingdom leisure centers are places where you can pursue your favorite sports or hobbies, and the same thing in the United States is called a recreation center!

- Ask the class for their understanding of the **Vocabulary** term *hobby* by asking them to list types of hobbies. There's probably little disagreement that collecting stamps, doing needlework, or creating scrapbooks are hobbies. What about shopping, hanging out with friends, or taking evening courses? Are these hobbies? Similarly, most would agree that a *chore* is a task that must be done regularly. Is it also something unpleasant and boring? A discussion on these topics makes students more aware of the shades of meaning in words.

- When the students do the word associations in **Vocabulary Skill** Part C, have them write down the words as they say them. Afterward, have them analyze any patterns they see. What were the connections? Was there an emotional tone to the connections, and if so, was it positive or negative?

- In **Real Life Skill**, point out that while it is useful to think of key words before you search, sometimes when you start using key words in a search engine, you discover others.

Extension Activities

Integrated Skill Extension: *Leisure Time Survey*

Students develop a survey questionnaire and ask their classmates about their leisure activities.

1. Explain that each student will develop a five-question survey about leisure. Brainstorm about the kinds of topics such a survey might include. Examples are: *amount of leisure time, leisure during weekends and holidays, favorite hobbies, favorite things to do with family, outdoor and indoor pursuits.* Consider dividing the topics so that each student is asking about something different.

2. Explain that students should design their questionnaire so that the answers will be easy to collect and analyze. Say that this is done by having a limited number of answers, such as the items at the beginning of the chapter. Have students write their questions and figure out how they will collect answers.

3. Tell students to circulate throughout the class, each asking ten different people their questions. The number ten is important because it makes it easy to talk about percentages of responses (e.g., if seven out of ten spend more than an hour a day online, then 70% do).

4. Have students write up their survey results and report on them to the class using either a pie chart or a bar graph to show some of their results.

Writing/Reading Skill Extension: *Five-Line Word Association Poem*

Students get additional practice with word associations by writing a five-line poem.

1. Explain that this simple poetry formula has appeared in many places. Note each line has certain requirements:
   line 1: 1 word, a noun
   line 2: 2 closely related adjectives
   line 3: 3 gerunds (verb+ing)
   line 4: a short, complete sentence
   line 5: a noun that is a synonym of the noun on line one

2. Write the formula on the board, go through it, and illustrate it with this example, which includes target vocabulary from unit 6:

   > Traffic   Hectic, stressful   Driving, sitting, waiting
   > Will I ever get home?   Commuting

3. Ask each student to write a poem, preferably on the themes of the unit.

4. Post poems on the wall and have their authors take turns reading them aloud.

Unit 7: A World of Music

Getting Ready

Answer Key

1. Sandor Nagy, classical; three guest DJs, dance music; Rockathon, rock; Jazz All-Stars, jazz; Salsa Party, salsa; One Love, reggae; Festival of Irish Music and Dance, Celtic

2. Answers will vary depending on personal taste and preference.

Chapter 1: Where's That Music Coming From?

Chapter Summary

Target Vocabulary: adapt, appealing, diverse, genre, influence, lyrics, rhythm, roots
Reading Skill: Predicting
Reading Passage Summary: Although different genres of music have their roots in particular places and circumstances, today many musical styles have become universal.
Vocabulary Skill: Prefix *ex-*

Answer Key

Before You Read

A: Answers will vary with likes and dislikes.

B: Other forms might include *world music*, *indie*, *opera*, or forms particular to their region such as *rai* for North Africa or *ragas* for India.

Reading Skill

A: Answers will vary according to guesses.

B: 1. Spain; **2.** Jamaica; **3.** India; **4.** Bob Marley; **5.** the U.S.; **6.** rhythm and blues

Reading Comprehension

A: 1. Bob Marley (lines 8–10); **2.** harvest, wedding (lines 12–13); **3.** dance floors (lines 16–18); **4.** Afro-American (line 19); **5.** white (lines 22–23)

B: 1. traditional (lines 12, 19–20); **2.** immigrants and travelers (lines 2–3); **3.** ordinary (lines 7–8); **4.** other countries (lines 28–31)

Critical Thinking

The author would probably agree with statements 1, 3, and 4.

Vocabulary Comprehension

A: 1. e; **2.** f; **3.** g; **4.** a; **5.** d; **6.** h; **7.** b; **8.** c

B: 1. influenced; **2.** roots, diverse; **3.** lyrics; **4.** genre

Vocabulary Skill

A: 1. exhausting; **2.** extended; **3.** extra; **4.** excited; **5.** experience; **6.** extensive; **7.** exclusive; **8.** expect

B: 1. exclusive; **2.** exhausting; **3.** excited; **4.** extensive; **5.** extended; **6.** extra; **7.** experience; **8.** expect

C: Some possibilities are: exactly, examination, excellent, exchange, expand, express.

Teaching Notes

- The genres or artistic categories of music mentioned in **Getting Ready** and **Before You Read** cover a wide range of music. It is difficult to categorize music because there have been so many cross influences, and some music, such as flamenco, fits into several categories. However, major categories are *classical*, *folk or traditional*, and *popular music*. *Classical* music concerts feature symphony orchestras, chamber groups, and solo instruments such as piano. *Folk music* is more informal and consists of music that has been handed down through the generations. *Popular music* includes jazz, rock, vocal, and many forms of dance music.

- Some of the dance forms mentioned in **Before You Read** are *hip-hop*, *rap*, *house,* and *techno*, which all have their roots in *electronic dance music*. This music is produced with electronic synthesizers and drum machines that supply a strong, steady rhythm. Although the forms originally were developed by urban youth, these types of dance music have become popular throughout the world.

Ask students about the genres of music mentioned on page 88.

- As students predict in the **Reading Skill** exercise, they may be unfamiliar with some names, but they should make guesses based on names and other background knowledge.
- Students will need to understand synonyms to answer item 3 in **Reading Comprehension**, Part B. They will need to recognize that *adapt* means "change" and that *average* is the same thing as *ordinary*.
- The **Critical Thinking** exercise requires inferencing.

For example, the author's agreement with statement 1 is implied, but it is also clear that many of the musical forms started years ago. Items 3 and 4 are not contradictory. In the past, music was spread by people traveling, but now and in the future, the Internet and mass media influence the spread of music around the world.

- In **Vocabulary Skill**, ask whether students can think of another meaning for the prefix *ex-*, which sometimes means "former," as in *ex-husband* or *ex-president*. Note that a hyphen is used.

Extension Activities

Writing/Reading Skill Extension: *Concert Review*

Students pretend they have attended a terrible concert and write a review of it.

1. Ask whether students have ever read reviews of concerts they attended. Did they agree with the opinion of the reviewer or critic? Why or why not? Brainstorm about words of praise and criticism that could be used in a concert review.
2. Ask students to pretend that they attended a concert that they found very disappointing. Explain that they should write a brief review, stating what they did not like and why.
3. Have students exchange their reviews with a partner and read them.
4. Ask if they could rewrite their review, is there anything they would change?

Integrated Skill Extension: *Battle of the DJs*

Groups of students have radio stations featuring DJs with different styles.

1. Activate background knowledge by asking students about their favorite DJs. What are their personalities like? What kinds of music do they play?
2. Explain that students will work in groups of four as different radio stations, each with a DJ. Point out that one person from each group will be chosen as the DJ, but the entire group will plan the program.
3. Have groups make a program featuring music from whatever genre they want and write a basic script for the DJ. But note that the DJ is allowed to improvise as well.
4. Let groups "rehearse" their programs before presenting them to the class. As happens in real life, the audience (the entire class) votes for their favorite DJ.

Optional Integrated Skill Extension: *We're Rapping*

Groups of students create and perform raps for the rest of the class.

1. Ask whether anyone is willing to demonstrate rapping or bring in a recording. Point out that the main features of rap are a strong underlying rhythm and rhyming lyrics.
2. Divide the class into groups of three students. Ask each group to create a short rap. The group should write out the lyrics and mark where the accents or stress marks are.
3. When groups have prepared their raps, ask each group to perform them for the rest of the class.
4. After each performance, note the rhythm and the rhyming patterns of the words.

Chapter 2: The Hot World of Salsa!

Chapter Summary

Target Vocabulary: classic, emigrate, incorporate, infectious, make a living, struggle, tempo, track

Reading Skill: Scanning

Reading Passage Summary: The dance music called salsa has its roots in the Spanish Caribbean, but today salsa is popular in Europe, Asia, and Africa as well as Latin America and North America.

Vocabulary Skill: Easily Confused Words

Answer Key

Before You Read

A: 1. Music with a strong beat or rhythm is good for dancing. **2.** Some of the Latin American music includes *tango, meringue, mambo, cha cha cha*, and *cumbia*. Popularity depends on the country, but *tango* is the most popular internationally. **3.** People hear new CDs on the radio or online. They are also promoted at live concerts. Reviews give opinions about new recordings and are available in newspapers, in magazines, and on the Internet.

Reading Skill

A: The artists on the recording include Celia Cruz, Ruben Blades, and Ricky Martin. La India is not mentioned in the review.

B: 1. 30; **2.** 1960s to today; **3.** very positive

Reading Comprehension:

A: 1. F, Puerto Rican, not Cuban (lines 9–10); **2.** F, jazz, not rock and roll (lines 15–16); **3.** T (lines 13–16); **4.** F, romantica, not caliente (lines 22–23); **5.** T (lines 25–29)

B: The order is 4 (lines 22–23), 1 (lines 11–12), 2 (lines 15–16), 5 (lines 30–34), and 3 (lines 20–21).

Critical Thinking

1. At least *great,* if not *excellent*
2. The word *great* is used three times, a track is described as *amazing,* and the final line ("sure to make you get up and dance") is very positive.

Vocabulary Comprehension

A: 1. a; **2.** b; **3.** b; **4.** b; **5.** a; **6.** a; **7.** a; **8.** a

B: 1. For better economic opportunities or for political reasons (warfare, famine, persecution); **2.** Answers will vary, but it should be a difficult subject. **3.** The question asks about a student's future job or career. **4.** Answers

will vary.

Vocabulary Skill

A: 1. immigrated; **2.** emigrated

B: 1. affect; **2.** effect; **3.** advice; **4.** advise; **5.** except; **6.** accept; **7.** than; **8.** then

Real Life Skill

A: 1. *hope*; the person wants to see Hiromi, but it is possible it might not happen; **2.** *looking forward*; school vacations are scheduled in advance, and the writer is eagerly anticipating the time off; **3.** Either *expect* or *hope* would work here: *expect* would be the better choice if the writer is confident that s/he will buy a piano; *hope* indicates that the writer has a strong wish or desire to buy a piano but is less certain that it will happen. **4.** *expecting*; Antonio has been on business trips before, and he is fairly sure what to expect.

B: Answers will vary. Make sure students explain to each other why they used each word.

What Do You Think?

Answers will vary. Some suggestions:

1. Immigrants bring many aspects of their home cultures with them, including music. Often these new genres of music become popular in the destination country.
2. In bilingual countries such as Canada or Belgium, singers sometimes make a political statement by singing in one of the languages. In some places, singers use a mixture of languages. For example, North African *rai* music is popular in Germany and sometimes sung in a mix of Arabic, Berber, and German.
3. Learning lyrics in English is a good way to practice stress and intonation in pronunciation. Some teachers use karaoke in their English classes to encourage students to learn English lyrics.

Teaching Notes

- The word *salsa* means "sauce" in Spanish. Some people believe that the same word is used for the food and the dance because both of them combine or *incorporate* many spicy components to produce something that is "hot" and pleasing.

- In the **Reading Skill** section, students are asked about the writer's opinion. Since scanning is the objective, they simply need to know that it is positive. Later, in the **Critical Thinking** section, they will have another question about the reviewer's opinion and will need to support their response with words from the text.
- The **Critical Thinking** questions require students to "read between the lines" to figure out the reviewer's opinion. Many reviews of movies and books also use a star system as a key to ratings, so students should consider what certain numbers of stars mean in terms of approval ratings. For example, if a movie gets three stars out of five, would it be worth seeing? When some stars aren't awarded, it pays to read a review carefully to understand some of the drawbacks.
- Both **Vocabulary** sections deal with the matter of *emigration/immigration*. Migration is a major social issue throughout the world, so it is important to understand the distinction. People are considered to *migrate* when they move permanently from one place to another. Therefore, when people travel on vacation or go to a place for a short time with the expectation of returning home, they have not migrated. Migration within a country is typically *rural to urban migration,* when people leave the rural countryside to live in cities. In developing countries, this is a serious matter because it places stress on city resources for public services, housing,

jobs, health care, and other resources. Emigration is either *voluntary*—when people choose to move—or *involuntary,* when they are forced to move against their will. Refugees from a war or famine are involuntary migrants. Poor immigrants who come to a wealthy country to find jobs are voluntary migrants.

- In the **Vocabulary Skill** and **Real Life Skill** sections, it is beneficial to use some memory strategies or word associations to keep the distinctions between the confusing words straight. Here are some that students find useful:
  - *Emigration/immigration:* remember that the prefix *im-* is another form of the suffix *in-*, so *immigration* means moving <u>in</u>to a place.
  - *Affect/effect: affect* is a verb and *effect* is a noun, so remember the phrase "cause and effect," which pertains to two nouns.
  - *Advise/advice: Advise* is a verb, *advice* is a noun. To remember which one is a noun, think: *It was ni<u>ce</u> advi<u>ce</u>.* The adjective *nice* goes with the noun *advice.*
  - *Accept/except: Accept* is only a verb meaning "to take something that is offered or to agree," so you are taking something <u>in</u>. *Except* can be several parts of speech (preposition, conjunction, or verb), but all the forms have the same basic meaning based on the prefix *ex-* (studied on page 91) with its important meaning of *out*.
  - *Except* comes from an old Latin word meaning *take out* or *exclude.*

Extension Activities

Speaking/Listening Skill Extension: *Dance Party*
Students discuss and demonstrate their favorite dances.
1. Ask students to tell about popular dances. Make a list on the board.
2. Ask for volunteers to demonstrate how to do some of the dances. Ask the volunteer to explain step-by-step how to do the dance. Remind the class that sequence markers are helpful!
3. Ask for other volunteers who do not know the dance but are willing to learn. The lead volunteer slowly repeats the steps while the others try to follow.

Writing Skill Extension: *A Migrant's Story*
Students write about someone who has permanently moved to a new location.
1. Ask students to think about people they know who have migrated (internally or internationally). Explain that they will write about the person's story. Brainstorm about factors that might be important, such as reasons for moving, ties with the old location, adjustment problems in the new location, etc.
2. Explain that if possible, students should try to ask these questions of the migrant and record the answers.
3. Each person writes an account of a migration of someone they personally know.
Note: Many students study English because they either have already migrated or have expectations of doing so in the future. Be respectful of students' accounts and do not require them to share their writing.

Unit 8: Career Paths

Getting Ready

Answer Key

1. From top left to bottom right: firefighter, doctor or nurse, office manager or secretary, chef, businessman, and flight attendant
2. Answers will vary. Overseas travel would be important for a flight attendant and perhaps a chef. Speaking a foreign language would be useful for a flight attendant, a businessman, and maybe even an office manager. Previous work or volunteer experience, and additional education or certificates, are both important for all jobs. A doctor, nurse, and businessman might all have university degrees.
3. Answers will vary.
4. Answers will vary.

Chapter 1: Be Your Own Boss

Chapter Summary

Target Vocabulary: advantage, balance, benefits, client, co-workers, invest, salary, schedule
Reading Skill: Identifying Main Ideas within Paragraphs
Reading Passage Summary: There are both advantages and disadvantages to having your own business, but most people enjoy the experience.
Vocabulary Skill: Compound Nouns

Answer Key

Before You Read
A: 1. Answers will vary. 2. **Advantages** include making your own decisions and setting your own schedule.
3. **Disadvantages** include paying for your own benefits, having a lot of responsibility, and taking financial risks.

Reading Skill
A: b
B: By paragraph numbers: 2. b; 3. a; 4. a; 5. b; 6. a

Reading Comprehension
A: **Advantages a.** how to do your work, how much money you want to make, who will work for you (lines 27–28); **b.** no limits (lines 32–33); **Disadvantages a.** bored or lonely (lines 15–16); **b.** schedule (lines 9–11); **c.** pay for your own benefits, like (lines 16–17); **d.** lose all the money you invested (lines 17–18)
B: 1. F, less than half of all businesses, *not* most (lines 18–19); 2. T (lines 16–17); 3. T (lines 12–13); 4. F, most enjoy the experience, not dislike it (lines 24–25).

Critical Thinking
Answers may vary, but most likely 2 and 3.

Vocabulary Comprehension
A: 1. f; 2. d; 3. e; 4. a; 5. b; 6. g; 7. h; 8. c
B: 1. schedule; 2. salary, benefits; 3. client, co-workers; 4. balance

Vocabulary Skill
A: No answers are needed, but make sure students understand the examples.
B: 1. police officer; 2. travel agent; 3. taxi driver; 4. car dealer; 5. hairdresser; 6. computer programmer; 7. firefighter; 8. office manager; 9. mail carrier; 10. bookkeeper
C: Answers will vary. Some possibilities: 1. police officer (courageous); 2. travel agent (experienced traveler); 3. taxi driver (knowledgeable about place, good driver); 4. car dealer (persuasive); 5. hairdresser (creative); 6. computer programmer (technologically skilled); 7. firefighter (strong, brave); 8. office manager (organized, efficient); 9. mail carrier (physically fit); 10. bookkeeper (accurate, good with details)

Teaching Notes

- In **Getting Ready**, as students think about the qualities that apply to particular jobs, it may be useful to put a matrix or chart on the board with job names in columns across the top and qualities in rows on the left side. Then have a class discussion about what qualities particular jobs require.
- Ask students about *gender stereotypes* they may have

about the jobs in the photographs. For example, how many of them thought the person with the stethoscope was a nurse instead of a doctor?

- For the **Reading Skill** of identifying main ideas, before students attempt Part B, ask them to skim the passage and circle the five most important words in each paragraph. These five words should be the "clues" to the main idea of the paragraph. Then ask them to complete Part B. Did identifying the key words help them to identify the main idea? Ask students to compare their answers with a partner and, using the words they circled, give reasons for choosing "a" or "b" as the main idea.

- In **Reading Comprehension**, the chart with *advantages* and *disadvantages* is actually a graphic organizer that can be used to evaluate many situations. To give students practice with this tool, ask them to go back to the jobs pictured in **Getting Ready** and list what they think are the *advantages* and *disadvantages* of each one. What kinds of careers are students considering? Have they thought of advantages and disadvantages in this way?

- One of the **Vocabulary Comprehension** words is *client*, someone who uses the services of a professional such as an accountant or a lawyer. Ask whether students can think of similar names for people who receive services. For example, *customer, patient, passenger, buyer*, etc.

- In **Vocabulary Skill**, students should note that sometimes two words are combined into one (*firefighter*), but sometimes they remain as separate words that have one meaning (*taxi driver*).

Extension Activities

Speaking/Listening Skill Extension: *Guess My Job*
Students tell characteristics of unusual jobs, and the rest of the class has to guess the job.
1. Have students work in groups of three. Tell each group to brainstorm unusual jobs and choose one to present.
2. Explain that the group must think of what the job entails in terms of actual work.
3. Have them take turns telling the class about three characteristics of the job. Have the rest of the class guess the job by asking no more than ten questions.
4. Note some examples of unusual jobs: *acupuncturist, tattoo designer,* and *zookeeper.*

Reading/Writing Skill Extension: *Dream Job Reality Check*
Students think of the ideal job and then do some research about it on the Internet.
1. In the first stage, have students think of their "dream job" and quickly write about it for five minutes, noting as much as they can about what the job requires. Explain that the writing will be collected but not reviewed.
2. Tell students to then research their dream job on the Internet (at http://jobprofiles.monster.com/ for example). Explain that they should learn what training or education is required, what the job actually is like, the average salary, and how competitive the field is. After taking notes on these factors, have students write a description of the job and why they are interested in it.
3. In class, let students compare the results of their research with their earlier writing. Have their feelings about their dream job changed? Explain why or why not.

Integrated Skill Extension: *Compound Occupations Scramble*
Students match compound names for occupations.
1. Have students work in groups of four to brainstorm compound names for occupations. Say that each group must find 15 names and write the words on separate small pieces of paper.
2. Scramble the pieces of paper, and have the groups time themselves while reassembling the names correctly. When all the names are reassembled, the group scrambles them again.
3. Have each group exchange its set of scrambled names with another group that does not have the advantage of having discussed the names. Let the new group reassemble the names, timing themselves. When they have finished, have groups compare their timing with the original group.

Examples: *travel guide, administrative assistant, bank teller, chemical engineer, disc jockey, interior decorator, news reporter, photojournalist, registered nurse, midwife, technical writer, truck driver, fisherman, social worker, dishwasher*

Chapter 2: The Right Job for Your Personality

Chapter Summary

Target Vocabulary: analyze, detail, emotional, interact, investigate, persuade, self-confident, solve
Reading Skill: Skimming for General Ideas
Reading Passage Summary: There is a strong relationship between personality and career choice as shown in six personality categories of people with particular jobs.
Vocabulary Skill: Adjective Endings

Answer Key

Before You Read

A: 1. Answers will vary. Some suggestions: nurse (kind, conscientious, observant); firefighter (risk-taking, responsible); actor (extrovert, adaptable); engineer (serious, disciplined); librarian (well-organized, creative); psychologist (sensitive, observant); salesperson (extrovert, enthusiastic); pilot (responsible, dependable, well-organized); athlete (self-confident, disciplined, competitive, persevering); kindergarten teacher (kind, responsible, outgoing)

Reading Skill

A: Students write three words to describe their own personalities.
B: Answers will vary.

Reading Comprehension:

A: 1. d (lines 26–27); **2.** e (lines 28–29); **3.** c (line 30); **4.** f (lines 31–32); **5.** a (lines 33–34); **6.** b (lines 35–36)
B: 1. F, most people are a combination of two or three types (lines 37–39); **2.** T (lines 26–27, 35–36); **3.** F, many people get their first job without really thinking about it (lines 1–2); **4.** F, true for Social type but not for Investigative (lines 28–29, 31–32)

Critical Thinking

Realistic: another "first responder" such as ambulance driver; **Investigative:** physicist, inventor; **Artistic:** dancer, figure skater; **Social:** therapist, gerontologist; **Enterprising:** newspaper editor, photojournalist; **Conventional:** bookkeeper, copy editor

Vocabulary Comprehension

A: 1. ignore; **2.** guess; **3.** make someone angry; **4.** self-confident; **5.** stay alone; **6.** main; **7.** ask; **8.** emotional
B: 1. detective, laboratory technician, investigative reporter; **2.** Convince them it is in their best interest. **3.** Do what you can do well until you build confidence. **4.** Answers will vary.

Vocabulary Skill

A: Students should circle the adjective endings of the example words.
B: 1. motivated; **2.** effective; **3.** interested; **4.** adventurous; **5.** aggressive; **6.** experienced; **7.** flexible; **8.** dynamic; **9.** enthusiastic
C: Answers will vary as students consider which jobs might be suitable for them.

Real Life Skill

A: 1. f; **2.** e; **3.** d; **4.** h; **5.** c; **6.** g; **7.** a; **8.** b
B: a. 2; **b.** 3; **c.** 1
C: Answers will vary.

What Do You Think?

Answers will vary. Some suggestions:
1. Students will have already done this as one of the activities for chapter 1. Ask whether there are personality factors that influence their opinion about the job.
2. Some reliable sources of information are school and university guidance counselors, newspaper articles, and Internet sites. Students should be wary of agencies and websites that charge money.
3. Answers will vary according to the country, the students' educational and experience level, and the job market.

Teaching Notes

• In **Before You Read**, students are asked to associate different personalities with particular jobs. Prior to doing this exercise, brainstorm about personality traits because some students may be unfamiliar with the vocabulary. Some of the positive terms are given in the **Answer Key**, but you may want to also elicit some <u>negative</u> ones such as *aggressive*, *cold* or *impersonal*, *emotional*, *impatient*, and *self-centered*. Other positive terms include *quiet*, *hardworking*, *original*, *independent*, *idealistic,* and *sociable*. Note that students will need to use personality vocabulary at several points in this chapter, so it is best to activate their knowledge at the beginning. For example, in **Reading Skill** Part A, they will have to supply three words to describe their own personalities.

- For the **Reading Comprehension** true/false questions in Part B, reinforce the **Reading Skill** of skimming for gist comprehension. Some of the answers are worded slightly differently from the questions, so tell students to look for ideas and not for exactly the same wording.
- Note that in psychology, *personality* refers to how a person behaves, thinks, and feels throughout their life, not just for one phase of it. Psychologists disagree about *personality types* beyond the basic types of *extrovert* and *introvert*. In the 20th

century many different theories of personality and personality tests were developed, each with strong supporters. One common test is the Meyers-Briggs Type Inventory (MBTI), based on the work of Carl Jung, which has 16 basic categories of personality types. This test has been used often in education and employment. See http://en.wikipedia.org/wiki/Personality_type for further information.

- In the **Critical Thinking** section, encourage students to "think out of the box" in extending the personality types to other occupations. However, for each suggestion, probe for reasons why that job might suit someone with the personality type.
- The vocabulary words are not highlighted in the **Reading Passage**, so ask students to find and circle each vocabulary item listed under **Vocabulary Comprehension**. Then ask students to discuss what each word means in the context of the reading.
- Discuss the categories in **Real Life Skill** Part A and ask for other jobs that fit in each category.

Extension Activities

Writing Skill Extension: *Personality Reflection*
Students think about their own personality and how it affects their lives.
1. After reading about personality types on page 103, have students identify which types are most like their own personality. Remind them that their personality may fit into several different groups, but that usually some characteristics are more important or dominant than others.
2. Have students write a journal entry on their own personality as they perceive it. For each trait, explain that they should give an example of how that characteristic works in their daily life.
3. Ask whether, based on their understanding of their own personality, there are things they would change. For example, would they seek out friends who have similar personalities or take advantage of some aspects of their personality by joining groups where that personality is an advantage? Are there other subjects they might study or new hobbies they might take up?
Note: This exercise is meant to be personal and reflective, so it would not be graded.

Speaking/Listening Skill Extension: *Guess Who?*
Students describe the personality of a classmate, and others guess who it is.
1. Have each student write ten words describing the personality of someone in the class who remains unnamed. Note that students can choose to write about themselves or the teacher.
2. Let each person take a turn at reading their description, being very careful not to give any clues (such as she/he pronouns) to the rest of the class.
3. The rest of the class has five guesses for each person.
4. If guessing proves difficult in some cases, note that sometimes outsiders have different perceptions of personality than a person does herself or himself. For example, the rest of the class may think someone is an extrovert because they participate a lot, but in fact, that person feels quite shy.

Getting Ready

Answer Key

1. Answers will vary depending on whether students like chocolate or not.
2. Some examples are desserts such as cake and ice cream, and drinks such as cocoa/hot chocolate.
3. Answers will vary. Common types of chocolate include milk, dark, white, and flavored (e.g., orange chocolate).

Chapter 1: The History of Chocolate

Chapter Summary

Target Vocabulary: adopt, consume, cultivation, currency, ingredient, invade, remain, rituals
Reading Skill: Skimming to Assess a Passage
Reading Passage Summary: Chocolate, first used about 3,000 years ago in Mesoamerica, spread to Europe through Spanish colonialism and today is loved throughout the world.
Vocabulary Skill: Identifying Part of Speech

Answer Key

Before You Read

A: 1. tree; 2. seeds; 3. the Americas; 4. drinking;
5. currency; 6. positive; 7. Spanish; 8. Africa

Reading Skill

A: 1, 2
B: 1. How chocolate evolved in the Americas, how explorers brought it to Spain, how it spread to France and later England and then throughout the world;
2. Mayan, Aztec, and Peruvian Inca chocolate drinks with chilies, Spanish sweetening of chocolate, and the English use of milk with chocolate

Reading Comprehension

A: 1. T (lines 8–11); 2. F, the drink was hot and spicy (lines 14–15); 3. T (lines 15–17); 4. F, it spread 100 years later (lines 27–31); 5. F, at first slaves were brought to the Americas (lines 35–36).
B: 1. a (paragraph 3); 2. a (lines 15–17, 28–30); 3. b (lines 14–15, 18–19, 25–26); 4. a (lines 6–8, 13–23, 36–38)

Critical Thinking

1. Bitter tasting. Opinions will vary.
2. Through marriage and migration of an important person. Yes, this is still common today.
3. The Spanish invaded the Philippines in 1565, a time when they had a monopoly or sole control of chocolate.

Vocabulary Comprehension

A: 1. a; 2. b; 3. a; 4. a; 5. a; 6. b; 7. b; 8. a
B: Answers will vary. Some suggestions: 1. New Year's or burial rituals; 2. pound, dinar, riyal, ruble, yen; 3. a skill such as weaving or painting, a friendship; 4. Many countries have experienced invasion.

Vocabulary Skill

A: 1. noun, a food item in a recipe; 2. adjective, something good or helpful; 3. noun, money or valuables
B: 1. extend over a wide area; 2. interest or need; 3. grown or farmed; 4. ceremonies

Teaching Notes

- **Getting Ready** asks about kinds of chocolate. Chocolate consists of cocoa butter and solids that can be easily melted during processing. Dark chocolate has about 70% chocolate solids, milk chocolate about 50%, and white chocolate only 33%. The processing of chocolate varies depending upon whether the end product is going to be eaten as candy or used as an ingredient.

- The **Reading Skill** of skimming and scanning quickly to assess a passage is very important in doing research, especially on the Internet. A simple search produces many results, and the next step is to decide whether any one site is useful for researching a particular topic. Such assessment requires that the reader has a clear idea of the topic and key words associated with the topic. While skimming or reading very quickly for gist comprehension, the reader is at the same time scanning for references to the topic or the key words. If, after skimming four or five articles, there doesn't seem to be anything that is close to the topic, it is better to search again using a different set of key words that perhaps will produce more "hits" or articles closer to the topic.

- In **Reading Comprehension** Part A, item 2, note that chilies are hot and spicy. Also, chocolate that has not been sweetened with sugar is quite bitter in taste. In fact, in the Aztec Nahuatl language, chocolate means "bitter water." To make this point, you might want to bring some unsweetened cooking chocolate to class for students to taste.

- For **Reading Comprehension** Part A, item 4, remind students that the century naming system runs 100 years ahead of the actual dates. Thus, the 17th century goes from 1600 to 1699 and the year 1700 starts the 18th century. Since the popularity of chocolate spread <u>after</u> it became popular in England around 1700, it happened in the 18th century instead of the 17th century. However, note that the **Reading Passage** says that the Spanish brought chocolate to the Philippines in the 16th century, meaning the 1500s.

- To sort out the sequence of events in the Reading Passage, ask students to work in pairs on a time line. In line 13, the text refers to 1000 B.C., meaning 1,000 years before Christ or the start of the present era of dates, also sometimes referred to as A.D. In lines 21–33, events proceed in chronological order, but note that the reference to the Spanish invasion of the Philippines will require going back on the time line to a little after the time of Cortez. Logically, Cortez had to bring chocolate to Spain before the Spanish could take it to the Philippines.

- In **Vocabulary Comprehension**, *adopt* refers to the process of deciding to use a thing or idea, as in the example "Mobile phone users were quick to adopt the new camera model," but it can also mean to legally raise an unrelated child as your own. Adoption is very common in some countries, but in countries in the Middle East, for example, it is not legally recognized.

Extension Activities

Listening/Speaking Skill Extension: *Chocolate Dreams*
Students work in small groups and describe their ideal chocolate dessert.
1. Have students work in groups of five or six so everyone has a chance to participate.
2. Have each person describe their ideal chocolate dessert. What are the ingredients? How would it be made? Have they ever had this dessert or is it just part of their imagination?
3. After the group listens to each person's description, have them vote for the best dessert.

Integrated Skill Extension: *Chocolate in the Media*
Students create a display of references to chocolate in songs, films, and books.
1. Have everyone brainstorm together about references to chocolate in songs, films, or books. Some examples are the Kylie Minogue song "Chocolate," the film and book titled *Like Water for Chocolate*, and the film *Willy Wonka and the Chocolate Factory*. Write the references on the board.
2. Divide students into as many groups as there are references. Have each group choose one reference and think of ways to make a poster about it. For example, if it is a film, who are the characters? Where is it set? When they have ideas, they make a poster.
3. Using a notice board or classroom walls, have students display their posters.

Reading/Writing Skill Extension: *Fair Trade Chocolate*
Students research chocolate production using the key words "fair trade chocolate" and write a report.
1. Explain that in recent years, a number of investigative reports (UNICEF, BBC, International Labor Organization, World Bank) have raised concerns that child labor is used in chocolate production. Tell students to find at least two sources of information on this topic by doing an Internet search with the key term "fair trade chocolate."
2. Have students take notes and write a brief report in which they state the problem and what is being done about it. Let them give their opinion and make suggestions about what people can do to improve the situation.
3. When students have prepared their reports, have a class discussion about the issues.

Chapter 2: *Addicted to Chocolate*

Target Vocabulary: addiction, chemicals, contribute, distinctive, equivalent, nutrition, release, stimulate
Reading Skill: Understanding Main Ideas within Paragraphs
Reading Passage Summary: Although the public thinks that chocolate causes health problems, research shows that these beliefs are not true and that chocolate actually can be good for health.
Vocabulary Skill: Synonyms

Answer Key

Before You Read

A: 1. Answers will vary. **2.** People think you might gain weight, have acne and cavities, and consume too much caffeine. **3.** *Addiction* is a psychological condition in which a person becomes dependent on consuming or doing something. People get addicted to alcohol, drugs, and smoking. **4.** *Addicted to Chocolate* indicates that people become dependent on eating chocolate.

Reading Skill

A: The sequence of main ideas is 6, 4, 5, 1, 2, and 3.
B: 1. No; **2.** Negative effects are balanced by positive ones.

Reading Comprehension:

A: 1. Eating chocolate usually makes people feel happy (lines 5–7); **2.** Chocolate contains chemicals that stimulate (or excite) the brain (lines 8–14); **3.** There is no real evidence that eating chocolate causes health risks (lines 15–36); **4.** It is a fact that chocolate contains saturated fat (lines 17–18); **5.** Eating chocolate doesn't cause tooth decay, so you can eat it without worrying (lines 28–31).

B: Positive effects: You feel better (lines 6–7), happier (lines 8–14); it contains phenolics, which can lower risk of heart disease (lines 20–23); it doesn't cause acne or tooth decay (lines 24–31). **Negative effects:** Chocolate contains saturated fat, which can contribute to bad cholesterol levels (lines 17–19); sugar added to chocolate can cause cavities (lines 31–32).

Critical Thinking

1. Answers will vary with opinions, but the question asks how often, so the answer should be a time such as daily, twice a week, once a month, etc.
2. It could increase chocolate sales and consumption.
3. Probably not, because there are other ways to achieve the same health benefits.

Vocabulary Comprehension

A: 1. b; **2.** f; **3.** d; **4.** a; **5.** c; **6.** h; **7.** g; **8.** e
B: 1. addiction; **2.** distinctive; **3.** stimulate; **4.** nutritional

Vocabulary Skill

A: 1. damaging: harmful; **2.** stimulate: energize, give a lift or high; **3.** proof: evidence; **4.** exercising: working out; **5.** quit: stop
B: 1. damaging; **2.** harmful; **3.** exercising; **4.** proof; **5.** stimulate; **6.** damage; **7.** evidence/proof; **8.** quit

Real Life Skill

A: 1. 2; **2.** 1; **3.** 2
B: Answers will vary, but students should use the first meaning of *consume* and *cultivate*, and the second meaning of *contribute*.

What Do You Think?

Answers will vary. Some suggestions:
1. Addictive substances and behaviors release chemicals in the brain that make people feel good, even though temporarily.
2. Coffee, tea, and beer are very popular throughout the world.
3. Note that some "essential" foods or drinks are important at particular times of the day. For example, some people do not feel awake without coffee in the morning.

• In **Before You Read**, students are asked about *addiction*. Addiction is seen as a negative situation where a person uses substances (such as tobacco, drugs, or alcohol) or engages in behaviors (such as gambling or impulse shopping) that are harmful to them. Ask the class about addictions. Which ones can they name?

- In **Reading Skill** Part B, students are supposed to base their answers solely on the main ideas given in Part A, not a close reading of the **Reading Passage**. Therefore, the reasons may focus on the reference to chemicals in main ideas 3 and 4.
- In **Reading Comprehension** Part A, all the sentences have mistakes. Encourage students to rewrite the sentences in their own words before checking the **Reading Passage**.
- For **Reading Comprehension** Part B, ask students to go back through the **Reading Passage** to underline positive effects and circle negative effects.
- Apropos the first **Critical Thinking** question, some doctors now recommend that people eat small quantities of dark chocolate (70% or higher cocoa content) daily.

Dark chocolate has more of the benefits and fewer drawbacks than milk or white chocolate.
- For **Vocabulary Skill** Part B, in principle, any of the synonyms could be used to fill a gap, but good writing style uses variety and avoids using the same word repeatedly.
- In **Real Life Skill** Part B, encourage students to write sentences with the other meaning of each word.
- In **What Do You Think**, question 1, be aware that some students might not want to talk about their experiences with breaking an addiction. Some efforts to break addictions, such as quitting smoking, are more "socially acceptable" for discussion than others such as resolving food disorders such as bulimia.

Extension Activities

Integrated Skill Extension: *It's Good for You!*
Small groups discuss foods and drinks that have been touted as "good for you."
1. Ask students to meet in groups of four. Have each group brainstorm about foods, drinks, or diets that they have heard are supposed to be healthy, such as green tea, red wine, the Mediterranean diet, oatmeal, grapefruit, etc.
2. Encourage students to discuss what they know about the special foods and the effects they are supposed to have.
3. Have individual students choose one of the foods/diets to research, looking for studies that have shown positive or negative results. Note how many people participated and for how long a time.
4. Tell students to report back to the rest of their group with their findings. They then compare their results with the other groups.

Speaking/Listening Skill Extension: *Non-food Addictions*
Students talk about behavioral addictions that are not associated with food.
1. Get students to brainstorm about behavioral addictions that do not concern food. Some examples are compulsive gambling, shopping addiction, excessive computer use, being a workaholic. Define such behavior as something that occurs to the extent that it is harmful to the addict in some way.
2. Ask why people become addicted to these behaviors. What are some of the characteristics or symptoms of such behavior? Are there any ways in which other people can intervene to stop the behavior or does the addicted person have to do that themselves?
3. Ask whether there are things in the culture or the society that contribute to the addiction. For example, some people become shopping addicts because they can get credit easily at first.

Writing Skill Extension: *New Year's Resolution*
Each person makes a journal entry about a skill or friendship they would like to cultivate.
1. Explain that New Year's resolutions mean things that people would like to change in their lives for the better.
2. Ask each person to write about something/someone they would like to know or understand better during the next year. How could they start to take action on this desire? If they are successful, how could it change their lives?
3. Point out that this activity is strictly personal, but in about a month, ask students to revisit their resolution.

Getting Ready

Answer Key

1. Answers will vary. Students *circle* the forms of advertising they encountered yesterday.

2. Students check or tick the advertising they actually read.

3. Students make note of any products they bought as a result of advertising they saw yesterday.

Chapter 1: *Ads Are Everywhere!*

Chapter Summary

Target Vocabulary: behavior, devise, global, logo, manufacture, put on, tiny, vehicle

Reading Skill: Skimming for the Main Idea

Reading Passage Summary: Although people are exposed to thousands of advertisements each day, they seldom think about the effect advertising has on their behavior.

Vocabulary Skill: Prefixes *in-, im-,* and *un-*

Answer Key

Before You Read

A: 1. Many locations are given in **Getting Ready**. **2.** After the term *slogan* has been defined with examples given, students individually make a list of slogans they know.

B: Students compare their locations for advertising and slogans. People remember slogans because they are short, "catchy," or memorable in some way, and because they see or hear them often.

Reading Skill

A: 1. F, thousands (line 1); **2.** T (lines 5–6); **3.** F, have used (line 9); **4.** T (line 16); **5.** T (line 25); **6.** F, think critically (lines 32–33)

Reading Comprehension

A: 1. N (lines 23–24); **2.** F (line 24); **3.** F (lines 27–28); **4.** N (line 19); **5.** N (line 20); **6.** N (lines 11–14)

B: 1. don't think much (lines 15–17); **2.** don't read the ad (lines 16–17); **3.** notice (lines 17–18); **4.** large (lines 25–28)

Critical Thinking

1. no; **2.** yes; **3.** yes; **4.** yes; **5.** no

Vocabulary Comprehension

A: 1. b; **2.** b; **3.** a; **4.** a; **5.** b; **6.** b; **7.** a; **8.** a

B: Answers will vary according to location, but students are probably familiar with some multinational examples.

Vocabulary Skill

A: 1. unaware; **2.** unbelievable; **3.** uncertain; **4.** incorrect; **5.** inappropriate; **6.** informal; **7.** unhappy; **8.** untidy

B: 1. uncertain; **2.** informal; **3.** inappropriate; **4.** no prefix; **5.** untidy; **6.** no prefix; **7.** unbelievable; **8.** unfortunately; **9.** inappropriate; **10.** no prefix

Teaching Notes

- In **Getting Ready**, ask students to answer the questions by themselves <u>before</u> they discuss them with a partner. After pair work, start a discussion about where and how they encountered or found this advertising. Ask why they read or paid attention to some ads and not others.

- **Before You Read** asks students to quickly think of *slogans*. Before students attempt this, explain that a *slogan* is a short saying that identifies a company's product or message. Give some examples from international companies, including:

  McDonald's *"I'm lovin' it"*
  Nike's *"Just do it!"*
  CNN's *"Be the first to know"*
  Intel's *"Intel inside"*

- In Part A of **Reading Skill**, students decide whether statements are true or false on the basis of skimming titles and the beginning of each paragraph in the reading. Remind the class that the first sentence of a paragraph is often, but not always, the topic sentence with the main idea for that paragraph. In Part B, ask students to underline the main ideas.

- For **Reading Comprehension** Part B, question 4, some students may answer "small" on the basis of the reference to tiny ads on apples in lines 23 and 24. This is an acceptable answer, but the verb phrase "trying to find ways . . ." indicates that companies are seeking new kinds of advertising, not things they have already done.
- For the **Critical Thinking** task, the author would be most likely to agree with statements 2, 3, and 4. Statement 1 is the opposite of the author's main point, and statement 5 is interesting but off-topic for this reading.
- Go over the **Vocabulary Comprehension** item *logo*, a design symbol for a company, product, or institution. Give examples that everyone knows, such as the McDonald's arches, the Microsoft Windows toaster, or the Red Cross/Red Crescent symbols. Logos are formatted in a special way, and they are copyrighted or legally protected so they cannot be used on products other than the proper brands. This could lead to an interesting discussion of copyright protection in your country and whether some famous brands are sold illegally as "knock-offs."
- In **Vocabulary Skill**, note that *inappropriate* can refer to behavior, clothes, and language. Just as you would not wear casual clothes for a formal occasion, you would not use informal language such as *slang* or *colloquialisms* during a formal speech. Ask about different situations that require particular behavior, clothes, and language to be appropriate.

Extension Activities

Integrated Skill Extension: *Reading Advertisements*
Students bring in print advertisements and analyze them.
1. Ask each student to bring in a print advertisement from a newspaper or magazine.
2. Have students work in groups of four and examine the ads for the product, the logo and slogan that indicate brand, and the messages that the ad presents.
3. Have students answer the following questions: Who is the intended or target audience for this ad (male, female, age, socioeconomic status, habits, lifestyle, etc.)? Do you think this ad is effective? Will you buy the product?
4. Encourage students to give detailed explanations.

Speaking/Listening Skill Extension: *Unwanted Advertising*
Students discuss unwanted and unsolicited (you didn't ask for it) advertising.
1. Brainstorm unwanted advertising with the class, such as spam, pop-ups, unsolicited faxes, and direct or junk mail. Make a list of these types of advertising on the board.
2. Discuss whether there is any value in advertising that you don't ask for or want to see. For example, does it make you aware of valuable products and services?
3. Ask students what they can do to stop unwanted advertising.
Note: Answers will vary, but you can block pop-up ads and spam with software, and you can put your name on lists not to receive junk mail.

Reading/Writing Skill Extension: *Public Service Advertising Log*
Students keep a log of public service advertising for one week.
1. Explain that public service advertising promotes an idea or service that is useful to society, not a commercial product. Point out that it is less common than paid advertising but is found on television, billboards, packaging, etc. Some examples are health advertising (AIDS prevention), emergency preparedness (what to do in major storms), and education (where to apply for scholarships).
2. Have students keep a log for one week in which they write a description of every public service advertisement they encounter. Tell them to note the purpose and sponsor of the ad as well as the location.
3. At the end of the week, have the class compare logs and create categories of public service ads.
Note: Public service ads will vary according to location and media exposure.

Chapter 2: How Advertising Uses Psychology

Chapter Summary

Target Vocabulary: aim, desire, elegant, image, product, react, slogan, vanity
Reading Skill: Distinguishing between Main and Supporting Ideas
Reading Passage Summary: The advertising industry uses psychology to sell products and create wants and needs.
Vocabulary Skill: Suffix -ist

Answer Key

Before You Read

A: A: 1. Answers will vary. Students should give a *reason* for liking the ad. **2.** Answers will vary. Note that the purchase of the product follows seeing an ad *once*.

Reading Skill

A: Paragraph 1: S, M; **Paragraph 2:** M, S; **Paragraph 3:** S, M

B: Paragraph 4: M: Advertisers use people's vanity to sell products OR Advertisers sell brands through selling images. S: watches with different personalities for each brand (watches), people paying more for designer brands; **Paragraph 5:** M: Advertisers use psychology to make their ads more effective. S: People feel positively about things they see often, so ads are used for a long time, people react better to ads that are repeated often.

Reading Comprehension:

A: 1. feelings or emotions (line 4); **2.** fear, love (line 4), enjoyment (line 15); **3.** effective (line 24); **4.** long (line 26), often (line 28)

B: 1. T (lines 4–11); **2.** T (lines 20–21); **3.** F, for the image (lines 22–23); **4.** F, they use psychology to understand how people respond (lines 25–28); **5.** T (lines 29–31)

Critical Thinking

1. vanity; **2.** fear; **3.** enjoyment, fun; **4.** fear, love; **5.** enjoyment

Vocabulary Comprehension

A: 1. b; **2.** f; **3.** d; **4.** e; **5.** h; **6.** a; **7.** g; **8.** c
B: 1. elegant; **2.** slogans; **3.** aim; **4.** product, image

Vocabulary Skill

A: 1. guitarist; **2.** biologist; **3.** numerologist; **4.** environmentalist; **5.** novelist; **6.** geologist; **7.** pianist; other occupations ending in -ist include dentist, artist, psychologist, physicist, flutist, violinist, etc.

B: 1. Any of the words could be used; **2.** probably a well-known person such as a pianist, guitarist, novelist; **3.** numerologist; **4.** novelist; **5.** numerologist; **6.** same as answer for 2

Real Life Skill

A: Students practice writing and speaking the numbers.

B: 1. 2,000,000; **2.** 4,500,000; **3.** 455,000; **4.** 1,728; **5.** 10,700

C: 1. four million six hundred thousand; **2.** two million three hundred thousand; **3.** four hundred (and) seventy-five thousand; **4.** one hundred (and) twenty-five thousand; **5.** eight thousand five hundred or eighty-five hundred; **6.** one million two hundred thousand or one point two million

What Do You Think?

Answers will vary. Some suggestions:

1. The word *catchy*, meaning memorable or attention-getting, is often given as a reason.

2. Some people object to advertising that destroys the atmosphere. For example, some states in the United States have banned billboard advertising from their scenic roadways.

3. Children have less ability to understand and resist advertising than adults, so they should not be shown advertising for things or behaviors that could be harmful.

Teaching Notes

- In the **Reading Skill** section, note that the main idea is found in the last sentence of paragraphs 1 and 3. Although the topic sentence containing the main idea is often the first sentence in a paragraph, a writer can give supporting details first and save the main idea until the end for effect. In paragraph 2, the supporting idea—*Some advertisements use fear to sell products*—is an example of the main idea of using people's emotions to sell products. Point out that some words are paraphrased from the reading. For example, in paragraph 1, *goal* is a synonym for *aim*. In paragraph 3, *fun and enjoyment* means *a good time*.

- The idea from paragraph 5 is referred to as an *advertising campaign*. Advertising campaigns are planned and organized to make people very aware of the product so they will buy it.

- In **Vocabulary Comprehension**, note that students are already familiar with *slogan* from the **Before You Read** section of chapter 1, where they had to brainstorm advertising slogans. Point out that *vanity* has a negative sense of being excessively proud of yourself, especially your appearance. It is related to the word *vain,* which comes from a Latin word meaning "empty, without substance." *Elegant* has a positive sense of being very stylish or refined, having good taste.

- *Image* can refer to an actual picture or one that is formed in the mind. Advertisers use specially designed photographs and drawings to help people create a certain positive mental image of their product. For example, a perfume ad might show a beautiful woman in a lovely garden. The mental image is of fragrant flowers and a romantic setting that you can experience if you use that perfume.

- In **Vocabulary Skill**, a *numerologist* is a person who studies patterns in numbers in order to make predictions and understand the supernatural.

- In **Real Life Skills**, note that different cultures have different ways of saying and writing large numbers. For example, some use periods or full stops instead of commas. In Britain a *billion* has 12 zeros, while in the United States a billion has only nine zeros!

Extension Activities

Integrated Skill Extension: *Slogan Fest*
Students analyze advertising slogans and share their results with the class.

1. Have the class brainstorm advertising slogans and write them on the board along with the name of the company or manufacturer and the product.
2. Point out that students can use http://en.wikipedia.org/wiki/Advertising_slogan for examples. Note that the website also has a list of criteria for effective slogans.
3. Have each student choose one slogan to analyze. Note that there should be enough slogans so that each student has a different one.
4. In their analysis, students should note why they think the slogan works by answering the following questions:
   What is the stated message?
   What does it suggest about the product or the company?
   What image of the consumer or buyer does the slogan create?
   Is the slogan clever or amusing in some way?
   What makes the slogan memorable?
5. Have each student present her/his analysis and see whether the rest of the class agrees.

Reading/Writing Skill Extension: *Hidden Advertising*
Students learn about two forms of hidden advertising and write about their experience with them.

1. Explain that sometimes advertisers hide their ads so that people are not consciously aware of them. Point out that two of the main ways of doing this are through product placement and subliminal advertising. Ask students to use these terms to research these types of advertising.

Note: *Product placement* is the presence of a logo or product in something that is not an advertisement. For example, it happens in films, television programs, and music videos. *Subliminal advertising* occurs when a very brief logo, picture of a product, or message is flashed during a film or television program. The event occurs so quickly that the viewer is unaware that it has really happened.

2. Tell students to gather information about hidden advertising and carefully note the sources of information that they use. Explain that in their reports, they should describe each form of hidden advertising, give examples, and then describe any personal experiences they have had with hidden advertising. Have them also give an opinion about whether they think this is a good idea or not, with support.
3. Have a class discussion about hidden advertising and its advantages and disadvantages.

Unit 11: Eating for Health

Getting Ready

Answer Key

Answers will vary. For **Healthy**, generally fruits, vegetables, and fish. For **O.K.,** generally meats, carbohydrates (bread, rice, pasta). For **Unhealthy,** everything with a lot of fat and/or sugar, such as butter, pizza, cookies, etc.

Chapter 1: Breakfast Like a King?

Chapter Summary

Target Vocabulary: boost, concentration, generally, heed, lethargic, mood, saying, wholesome
Reading Skill: Making Inferences
Reading Passage Summary: Nutrition experts say that having a healthy breakfast and eating your main meal earlier in the day give your body the energy it needs.
Vocabulary Skill: Word Families

Answer Key

Before You Read

A: 1. Answers will vary. **2.** "An apple a day . . ." means that you can prevent getting sick by eating healthy food. "You are what you eat" means that food provides the material your body needs to maintain itself. **3.** Answers will vary depending on country. **4.** We can guess or infer that there is a connection between James's diet and his heart attack.

Reading Skill

A: 1. b; **2.** lines 25–30 on the Swiss diet
B: 1. a; **2.** c

Reading Comprehension

A: 1. breakfast (lines 11–18); **2.** earlier (lines 19–20); **3.** several times a week (lines 28–30); **4.** the U.S. (lines 21–24)
B: 1. F, quite varied, not similar (lines 33–34); **2.** T (lines 19–20); **3.** F, breakfast, not dinner (lines 14–17); **4.** T (lines 31–37)

Critical Thinking

1 and 5 are healthy and maybe 4, depending on the soup. To make more nutritious: **1.** add fruit; **2.** add protein and fruit; **3.** add carbohydrates (cereal, bread) and protein; **4.** If soup has protein and carbohydrates it could be okay.

Vocabulary Comprehension

A: 1. daydreaming; **2.** book; **3.** lower; **4.** harmful; **5.** ignore; **6.** diet; **7.** energetic; **8.** rarely
B: 1. mood; **2.** boosts; **3.** concentration; **4.** wholesome

Vocabulary Skill

A: nutrition and nutrient (nouns), no verb; consumer, consumption (nouns), consumer (also adjective); digestion (noun), digestible (adjective); concentrate (noun and verb), concentration (also adjective); no verb form, moody (adjective), boost (noun and verb), booster (adjective)
B: 1. digestion, concentration; **2.** suggestion; **3.** mood; **4.** concentrate; **5.** boosts; **6.** concentration; **7.** consumption; **8.** moody; **9.** suggest
C: Answers will vary.

Teaching Notes

- In **Getting Ready**, encourage discussion about the categories for the foods listed. In general, nutritionists believe that several servings of fruit and vegetables should be part of the daily diet, but other foods should be eaten in moderation with careful attention to food values. Health experts disagree about the benefits and drawbacks of coffee and tea as well as chocolate (see unit 9). Bacon, sausage, and pizza all contain large amounts of saturated fat, as does some ice cream. They have high calorie value compared to the percentage of healthy nutrients. French fries (or chips in Britain) are especially unhealthy if they have been cooked in trans fats.

- Healthy food is a very controversial topic, with news articles almost daily that claim that some food that was considered unhealthy is now good for you. Making sense of the food claims is part of critical thinking. See http://www.hsph.harvard.edu/nutritionsource/media.html for some suggestions about interpreting food news. The Harvard School of Public Health website also has a wealth of useful information about food and health.

- The **Reading Skill** of making *inferences* means that students have to go beyond what is actually stated for ideas that are implied or suggested by what is written. Some people call this "reading between the lines" for opinions, attitudes, or even logical deductions. For example, in Part B, item 2, the reader can guess that the Mexican meal takes an hour or more because of the amount and variety of food that appears in different *courses*. In some parts of the world, different parts of a meal are served in order or sequence, not all at once. When diners have finished a course, the table is cleared before the next course is served. The list of Mexican foods includes an appetizer (something eaten before the main meal), soup, pasta, a fish course, a meat and salad course, a dessert, and, after the dessert is finished, coffee or tea. Eaten in order, the meal would take an hour.

- Be aware that in other cultures, the entire meal appears on the table at one time and there are no distinctions between different courses. Diners can help themselves to any dish in any order.

- In the **Reading Passage** and **Critical Thinking**

sections, note that meals differ in each country. In some Asian cultures, breakfast consists of a substantial soup with many healthy ingredients added for nutrition and flavor. Examples are *congee* rice soup (China, Thailand), *pho* (Vietnam), and *miso* soy soup (Japan). Also, "dinner" is not necessarily the evening meal.

- In **Vocabulary Comprehension**, *lethargic* is a powerful, low-frequency word that would only be used to describe an unusual situation. It means that someone is very slow and not alert, due to exhaustion or illness or as the result of medications. When someone inquires "How are you today?" it would not be appropriate to answer "Lethargic."

- In **Vocabulary Skill**, some word forms will remain the same although they are different parts of speech. *Consumer* is a noun, but in phrases such as *consumer confidence* and *consumer goods*, it is an adjective. *Concentrate* is a verb, but also a noun as in *orange juice concentrate*. *Concentration* is a noun, but sometimes it is an adjective as in *concentration camp*. *Mood* is also used as both a noun and an adjective. Your *mood* may improve with *mood music* or get worse with *mood swings*. *Boost* means to improve, increase, or push from below, so you can *boost* your energy (verb) or get a *boost* from caffeine. The adjective form really shows the "push from below" sense in *booster seat* (something that makes a child sit higher) or *booster rocket* (a rocket that helps a space shuttle get off the ground). Point out that many of these phrases are *collocations*, words that often occur together.

Extension Activities

Reading/Writing Skill Extension: *Reading Food Values*
Students read labels of five of their favorite foods.
1. Explain that many foods come with nutrition facts on the package or label. Tell students that they will read the labels of five of their foods, compare them with other brands, and decide whether to eat them based on the nutritional information.
2. Make sure students keep a record of the information and their choices.
3. For each of the five foods, have them write about their choices and the food values.

Speaking/Listening Skill Extension: *Fast Food*
Students discuss the advantages and disadvantages of fast food.
1. Make columns on the board for advantages and disadvantages of fast food.
2. Ask the entire class to brainstorm their ideas about fast foods. Ask students to give specific examples to support their opinions.
3. Ask for some strategies to take advantage of the good qualities of fast food while minimizing the disadvantages. For example, order salads and ask to have fattening dressings left off.

Chapter 2: *Is Your Diet Destroying the Environment?*

Chapter Summary

Target Vocabulary: crop, deficient, efficient, estimate, exclude, expel, livestock, vital
Reading Skill: Understanding Cause and Effect
Reading Passage Summary: A vegetarian diet is better for personal health and for the environment.
Vocabulary Skill: Root Word *vit/viv*

Answer Key

Before You Read
A: Answers will vary according to personal habits. Tally scores with three points for each "a" answer, two points for each "b," and one point for each "c" answer.

Reading Skill
A: 1. b; **2.** d; **3.** e; **4.** a; **5.** c
B: A meat diet can have these negative effects on the environment: **1.** it uses more water; **2.** it creates more methane gas; **3.** it produces less food per acre than if plants were grown.

Reading Comprehension:
A: 1. Vegetarians are less at risk for heart disease and other serious illnesses (lines 2–3). **2.** Eating meat is bad for the environment because livestock animals produce methane gas (lines 19–25). **3.** It is possible to produce more vegetables than meat on one acre of farmland (lines 14–18). **4.** Nutritionists believe that following a diet without any animal protein is not always healthy (lines 28–31). **5.** According to the reading, there are now too few vegetarians (entire reading).
B: 1. b (line 2); **2.** b (line 22); **3.** a (lines 12–14); **4.** b (lines 15–18); **5.** b (lines 30–31)

Critical Thinking
Answers will vary according to personal opinion. Some possibilities: **1.** vegetarians have lower risk of disease, and their diet has less impact on the environment (uses less water, gives off less methane gas, is more efficient). **2.** Answers will vary. **3.** As the number of people on earth increases, the amount of land remains the same so it has to be used more efficiently. Therefore, more people may have to become vegetarian.

Vocabulary Comprehension
A: 1. g; **2.** b; **3.** a; **4.** f; **5.** d; **6.** h; **7.** e; **8.** c
B: 1. exclude; **2.** deficient; **3.** estimate; **4.** vital

Vocabulary Skill
A: vitamin: noun, a substance necessary for health and nutrition; **survive:** verb, to live through something difficult and not die; **revive:** verb, to bring something back to life or to its full strength; **vitality:** noun, liveliness; **vivacious:** adjective, lively and high-spirited; **vivid:** adjective, very clear or intense
B: 1. survived; **2.** vitamins, vitality; **3.** vivacious; **4.** vitamin; **5.** revive; **6.** vivid
C: Answers will vary. Each sentence should include at least one word from the chart.

Real Life Skill
A: 1. weight; **2.** length; **3.** liquids, volume; **4.** distance; **5.** temperature; **6.** land area
B: 1. pounds, gallon, pounds; **2.** Fahrenheit; **3.** miles; **4.** feet, inches, pounds; **5.** miles, gallons; **6.** acres
C: 1. 10–12; **2.** has the flu; **3.** takes a bus; **4.** overweight; **5.** doesn't need; **6.** big

What Do You Think?
Answers will vary. Some suggestions:
1. Eat more fruits, vegetables, and whole grain cereal products.
2. As a result of fast food, many people have become seriously overweight or obese.
3. More foods may become organically grown or genetically modified.

Teaching Notes

- In the **Before You Read** questionnaire, *junk food* means food with a high calorie value because it contains a lot of fat or sugar or both, but relatively little real food value.

- In **Reading Skill**, ask students to match up the causes and effects by themselves, then discuss the matches with a partner. They should be able to give logical reasons for their choices.

- **Reading Comprehension** Part A, item 5, requires making an inference because the reading never states anything directly about there being too many or too few vegetarians.
- In **Vocabulary Comprehension**, *expel* has the sense of putting someone or something out with a certain amount of force. Example: *After his third warning for cheating, the principal expelled Charlie from the school. Charlie was told he would never be able to return.* On the other hand, if you *exclude* someone, you just leave them out; no force is used. Example: *Nina realized she was excluded from Carla's birthday party when all the other girls had plans for that afternoon.*
- The word *vital* means essential, crucial, needed for life, so a person's *vital signs* are heartbeat, respiratory (breathing rate), and temperature.

- In **Vocabulary Skill**, students may recognize two words: *viva* and *curriculum vitae*. In the United Kingdom and other places, students have a *viva*, a live interview in which they are asked questions instead of an exam. Throughout the world, a resume of your education and work experience is called a *curriculum vitae*, a document that tells about the course of your life.
- In **Real Life Skill** Part C, students are required to use their inferencing skills to answer the questions. If they find it challenging, refer them to the table at the top of page 144 and ask them to figure the amounts with metric measurements. Point out that non-metric measurements are primarily used in the United Kingdom and the United States.

Extension Activities

Writing Skill Extension: *Food Log*
Students keep a food log for a week, including everything they eat and drink.
1. Explain that many people estimate that they eat and drink very differently than they actually do. For the first step in this activity, ask each student to write down everything they ate or drank yesterday.
2. Explain that for the next week, they will keep a notebook with them and write down everything they eat or drink and answer these questions:
   What type of food or drink did they consume?
   How much of it did they eat or drink?
   When and where did this happen (at home, at a restaurant, on the street, between meals, etc.)?
   Why did they eat or drink each time (mealtime, at a party, a snack while watching TV)?
3. At the end of a week, have students analyze their food log for good and bad patterns.
4. Ask students to compare their estimate of what they ate with their food log. Which is accurate?

Integrated Skill Extension: *Vegetarian for a Day*
Students follow a vegetarian diet for a day and note any issues.
1. Explain that in some cultures it is not easy to be a vegetarian because small amounts of meat or fish appear in most dishes. Tell students you want to make them more aware of vegetarianism by having them give up all meat and fish for a day. Have them take notes about any special steps they had to take, such as asking about ingredients, eating foods they usually avoid or ignore, or finding that they need to eat different amounts.
2. After everyone has tried the one-day experiment, have a discussion about their experiences. Ask if they chose to become vegetarians, what would they do differently from now (take vitamins, eat more soy products, etc.)?

Reading/Writing Skill Extension: *Research Methane Pollution*
Students research methane pollution and report on ways to reduce it.
1. Note that prior to this chapter, some students may not have been aware of methane pollution. Explain that this serious environmental hazard comes from many sources other than just livestock: from decaying rubbish in landfills, coal mining, grassland or forest fires, and even from rice production! Ask students to find out more about methane pollution from the Internet.
2. Ask each student to suggest ways to reduce methane pollution. Have groups of students work together on posters that make other people aware of the ways methane pollution can harm the environment.

Unit 12: Saving the Environment

Getting Ready

Answer Key

Answers will vary. After thinking about how they could change "sometimes" or "never" answers, have students discuss their responses with a partner.

Chapter 1: Clean Up Australia, Clean Up the World

Chapter Summary

Target Vocabulary: ambitious, enormous, participate, pick up, represent, restore, specialize, volunteer
Reading Skill: Scanning for Numbers
Reading Passage Summary: Ian Kiernan's environmental clean-up program in Sydney Harbour became a nationwide movement in Australia and then a global program.
Vocabulary Skill: Prefix re-

Answer Key

Before You Read

A: Answers will vary according to opinions and where students live. Some possibilities: **1.** Some cities have stronger laws against pollution and more efficient public transportation systems than others; **2.** People can organize clean-up and recycling programs, politicians can create laws that protect the environment. **3.** People can join groups to make the public more aware of problems, they can get petitions to show support for changes, recycling centers, or greater reuse of household items.

Reading Skill

A: 1. 1989; **2.** 40,000; **3.** 8,450; **4.** 20 percent; **5.** 1993; **6.** 30 million (30,000,000); **7.** 80

B: 1. 18 years (by 2007); **2.** successful, effective; **3.** They covered a larger area and involved more people.

Reading Comprehension

A: The order is: 4 (lines 12–13), 1 (lines 2–4), 5 (lines 15–22), 6 (lines 30–37), 3 (lines 7–9), 2 (lines 5–6).

B: 1. a (line 4); **2.** c (lines 15–19); **3.** c (lines 26–29); **4.** b (lines 33–34)

Critical Thinking

Answers will vary. Some suggestions: **1.** It may depend on how aware people are of environmental issues and whether they feel they can do something about them; **2.** They can create awareness of problems and change people's habits.

Vocabulary Comprehension

A: 1. b; **2.** a; **3.** b; **4.** a; **5.** a; **6.** b; **7.** b; **8.** a

B: Answers will vary. Some possibilities: **1.** a house, furniture, a car; **2.** Rotary International, Doctors Without Borders, Habitat for Humanity; **3.** to become a political leader, a famous film star, win a prestigious scholarship; **4.** take part in discussions and small group work, ask questions, bring in additional material to share with the class.

Vocabulary Skill

A: reasons, recycle, recyclables, review, reduce, recycle, return, recyclables, receive, refund, repair, recycle, recycling

B: 1. repair; **2.** recyclables; **3.** reduce; **4.** recycle; **5.** refund; **6.** receive; **7.** review

C: Answers will vary. Some suggestions: react, readjust, reappear, rebirth, rebuild, recall, recur, reelect.

Teaching Notes

- Before asking students to take the quiz in **Getting Ready**, ask the class to brainstorm about ways they can help the environment. Note that there is a difference between *reusing*, where items are used again in the same form, and *recycling*, where items are processed in some way to get some value back from the raw material. If you use a plastic shopping bag again you are not changing it, but if you put a plastic water bottle into recycling, it is melted down and made into something else.

- In **Reading Skill**, point out that students will actually scan for key words, not for numbers, because they won't know which numbers to look for until they find

them with the terms. Before they scan for answers, ask students to underline a maximum of three words in each line as the words they will use for searching. For example, the words for the first item would be *first*, *Sydney,* and *Harbour.*

- The **Reading Skill** box mentions numbers and statistics. *Statistics* are not just numbers: they are numerical information that has been processed and analyzed. For example, *percentages* tell about the proportion of a population that recycle, not just the numbers of people who practice recycling.

- In **Reading Comprehension** Part B, item 2, students have an opportunity to practice inferencing skills. Although the **Reading Passage** does not mention either cities or countryside by name, line 19 mentions "beaches, parks, streets, and waterways," so ask students where these places are located. To answer item 4, students must realize that *weekend* is a way to paraphrase two days. Note that reading should focus on meaning, not exactly the same words.

- The **Reading Passage** says that 8,450 *tons* of garbage were collected during Clean Up Australia Day in 2005. In the United States, a *ton* is 2,000 pounds or the equivalent of 907 kilograms. A *ton* is heavier in the United Kingdom, weighing in at 2,240 pounds or 1,016 kilograms. Ask students who use the metric system to compute how many kilograms of garbage were collected.

- **Vocabulary Skill** emphasizes the prefix *re-*, but not all words that start with *re-* have the meaning of doing something again. See the activity below for opportunities to make the distinction.

Extension Activities

Vocabulary Skill Extension: *Which* re- *words mean "do it again"?*
Students use dictionaries to find words starting with *re-* and deciding whether they mean "again."

1. Remind students that some words starting with the letters "re-" do not mean to do something again. Give words such as reason, recent, read, regular, and reign as examples.
2. Ask students to work in groups of four or five. Explain that their task is to use a dictionary and make two lists of words they recognize. One list is those words in which the *re-* prefix means "again," and the other list is words in which *re-* is part of a different root word.
3. Give each group an opportunity to read off its list of words. Have the other groups check or tick the words that appear on their lists.
4. If students disagree about which list a word belongs to, ask them to look at the origin of the word.

Reading/Writing Skill Extension: *Garbage Log*
Students keep a log of everything they throw away for three days and then think about what they could do differently.

1. Say that people are often amazed to see how much garbage or rubbish they generate. Explain that this activity is designed to raise awareness.
2. For three days, have students make note of <u>everything</u> they throw away, from snack wrappers to printer cartridges. Have them also note where they put the waste.
3. At the end of the period, have students review their lists and think of things that could have been recycled or reused. Are there things that could have been disposed of differently? For example, were batteries or household chemicals properly disposed of so they couldn't harm the environment? Are there places to recycle aluminum, glass, paper, and plastics?
4. Have each student make a list of ways to manage waste better.

Chapter 2: Resources for the Future

Answer Key

Before You Read

A: A: 1. Answers will vary, but some additional suggestions are coal, petroleum, natural gas, forests, minerals, and fish. **2.** Students circle natural resources that are plentiful and underline those that are either scarce now or will be in the future.

Reading Skill

A: Only the second item (*where rainforests are located*) is not contained in the reading.
B: 4, 5, 1, 3, 2, 6

Reading Comprehension

A: 1. Scientists are now very worried about two of the Earth's most important resources (lines 2–4). **2.** Water pollution, overpopulation, and deforestation are the causes of dwindling water supplies (lines 11–13). **3.** Grain harvests in India will decrease because of water shortages (lines 13–14). **4.** Rainforests are important because they put out oxygen and provide us with medicine (lines 21–25). **5.** Lowering people's consumption of meat can help to save the rainforest (lines 30–32).
B: 1. check both (paragraphs 1, 3, and 5); **2.** water shortage (lines 11–13); **3.** check both (lines 16–17, 28–29); **4.** rainforest loss (paragraph 4); **5.** water shortage (lines 11–12, 14–16)

Critical Thinking

1. and **2.** In both cases, the author is trying to show the importance of the natural resources and build a case for conserving them. **3.** Maybe wind, tidal power, and solar energy, all renewable resources.

Vocabulary Comprehension

A: 1. b; **2.** g; **3.** f; **4.** a; **5.** e; **6.** c; **7.** d; **8.** h
B: 1. major; **2.** a solution; **3.** an endangered; **4.** a shortage

Vocabulary Skill

A: 1. d; **2.** a; **3.** b; **4.** c; **5.** e
B: 1. a; **2.** c; **3.** d; **4.** b; **5.** e
C: Answers will vary.

Real Life Skill

A: 1. d; **2.** e; **3.** g; **4.** c; **5.** f; **6.** b; **7.** a
B: 1. DVD; **2.** PC, CD; **3.** ASAP; **4.** URL; **5.** FAQ; **6.** CV
C: Answers will vary, but they should include at least one acronym per sentence.
D: Other common acronyms include ATM (automatic teller machine) and a.m./p.m. (ante and post meridian, Latin for before noon and after noon).

What Do You Think?

Answers will vary. Some suggestions:

1. If the place is unspoiled, ask why it is not affected by environmental problems. Is it a protected area? Is it very far from where most people live?

2. Population growth is a major factor in thinking 20 years into the future because our supplies of air, water, and many plants and animals will not increase. However, ask about examples of once endangered species that are now out of danger.

3. What can individuals do about global warming and greenhouse gas emissions?

Teaching Notes

- In **Before You Read**, students are asked to list *natural resources*. There are two main categories of natural resources. *Renewable resources* are things such as wood from forests or fish from the sea that can regenerate as long as people don't use them at a rate higher than the replacement rate. *Non-renewable resources* include oil, coal, natural gas, and minerals. These were formed in the earth over millions of years. Once they are used, they are gone forever.

- The **Reading Skill** of skimming to decide whether a passage is on topic or not is crucial for using the Internet. Search engines produce so many results that students need to be able to quickly identify ones that are useful for their purposes. In addition to finding information, they also need to make sure it is at an accessible level, not too technical or too simple. Furthermore, they need to decide whether the source is trustworthy.

- In **Reading Comprehension** Part A, sentence three, note that three changes are necessary. The tense needs to be changed from past to future, *increase* needs to become *decrease,* and *supplies* must be changed to *shortages.*

- Several items in **Vocabulary Comprehension** warrant attention. Students tend to confuse *dangerous* (capable of causing harm) with *endangered* (plants or animals that could become extinct because they are so rare). Write the two words on the board and ask for examples in each category. Are there some plants or animals that fit both categories?

- *Dwindle* has the sense of decreasing little by little, sometimes so gradually that it is not noticeable.

- Ask students to make connections between *pharmaceutical* and *pharmacy,* a place that sells medicine. In the United States a pharmacy is sometimes called a *drugstore,* and in Britain it is known as a *chemist*.

- In **Real Life Skill** on acronyms, note that some acronyms are spelled out as separate letters, such as IBM for International Business Machines. Others are pronounced as though they were a word, for example, NATO (for North Atlantic Treaty Organization) is pronounced "nay-toe," not "N-A-T-O."

Extension Activities

Writing/Reading Skill Extension: *Letter to the Editor*
Students write letters to an editor suggesting a solution to an environmental problem.
1. Brainstorm with the class about environmental problems that affect their daily lives.
2. Have students choose one of the problems and write a brief letter to a newspaper editor. In the letter, have them explain why people should take action now and then suggest something individuals could do to make things better.
3. Note that if students live on campus, the problem should be something that affects daily life as well as something that could be effectively dealt with by students. For example, if litter is a problem, propose a campus clean-up day.
4. Have students read drafts of each other's letters and give constructive feedback.

Real Life Skill Extension: *Text Messaging Acronyms*
Students develop a dictionary of acronyms for text messaging.
1. Divide the class into five groups, each responsible for a range of alphabet letters. Group 1 gets A–E, group 2 has F–J, group 3 has K–O, group 4 gets P–T, and group 5 has U–Z.
2. Explain that each group is responsible for brainstorming acronyms used in text messaging and putting them in alphabetical order. Examples are BTW for "by the way" and NOYB for "none of your business."
3. Have each group write a text message containing at least ten of the acronyms they have documented. Other groups try to read the message. Point out that if they need help, they can refer to the list.
4. Have the class put the combined list together and add items as they are encountered.

Review Unit 1

Question Section
Answers will vary, but expect students to provide two or three questions for their reading based on the survey activity. The questions will provide a reason for reading.

Word Web Answers
1. three (3); **2.** parents; **3.** tests; **4.** educational styles; **5.** vocabulary; **6.** problem solving

Fluency Reading: Are Human Beings Getting Smarter?

Answer Key

B. Reading Comprehension
1. b (lines 4–5); **2.** b (lines 6–10); **3.** c (lines 6–7); **4.** a (lines 11–18);
5. b (lines 15–17); **6.** a (lines 25–28); **7.** d (lines 25–29)

Self Check: PRO Strategy

Personal Responses to Reading Strategy
Individual students will have different responses to
the self check questions. The questions are meant to
encourage reflection on the reading process.

Review Reading 1: Fair Trade Chocolate

Answer Key

Reading Comprehension
1. a (lines 1–3); **2.** c (line 4); **3.** a (lines 6–7); **4.** b (lines
12–14); **5.** b (lines 10–12); **6.** b (line 17), c (lines 19–20);
7. a (lines 23–27)

Review Reading 2: A Different Kind of Spring Break

Answer Key

Reading Comprehension
1. c (lines 2–4); **2.** c (entire reading passage); **3.** a
(line 6); **4.** c (lines 9–17); **5.** d (lines 11–17); **6.** a (lines
22–23); **7.** a (lines 25–27)

Review Unit 2

Question Section
Answers will vary, but expect students to provide two or three questions for their reading based on the survey activity. The questions will provide a reason for reading.

Fluency Reading: *Movies for the Blind?*

Answer Key

Reading Comprehension:
1. b (entire article); 2. d (lines 4–6); 3. c (paragraph 2, especially lines 12–17);
4. c (line 18); 5. a (lines 24–31); 6. a (lines 32–34); 7. b (lines 42–46)

Self Check: *PQR+E*

Personal Responses to Reading Strategy
Individual students will have different responses to the self check questions. The questions are meant to encourage reflection on the reading process.

Review Reading 3: *Meet Freddy Adu, Soccer Sensation*

Answer Key

Reading Comprehension
1. c (lines 4–6); 2. d (lines 4–7); 3. a (lines 7–8); 4. b (lines 11–12); 5. b (lines 4–5); 6. d (lines 20–22); 7. c (lines 25–26)

Review Reading 4: *Combining New and Old Medicine*

Answer Key

Reading Comprehension
1. d (entire article); 2. a (lines 9–12); 3. d (integrative medicine is mentioned on lines 10–11); 4. a (line 16); 5. c (line 20); 6. c (lines 24–28); 7. b (lines 29–34)

Question Section

Answers will vary, but expect students to provide several things they already know about the topic as well as things they would like to learn. The things they want to learn will provide a reason for reading.

Fluency Reading: Geocaching

Answer Key

Reading Comprehension:
1. d (lines 4–10); 2. b (lines 2–10); 3. a (lines 4–8);
4. c (lines 16–21); 5. b (lines 5–7); 6. c (lines 18–19);
7. a (lines 22–23) and d (inference from entire article)

Self Check: KWL

Personal Responses to Reading Strategy

Individual students will have different responses to the self check questions. The questions are meant to encourage reflection on the reading process.

Review Reading 5: The People Behind the Music

Answer Key

Reading Comprehension
1. c (entire article); 2. a (lines 2–3, 26–29); 3. a (lines 10–12); 4. b (lines 10–12); 5. d (lines 14–17); 6. b (lines 22–24); 7. c (entire article)

Review Reading 6: Is It Time to Change Jobs?

Answer Key

Reading Comprehension
1. c (entire article); 2. a (lines 5–9); 3. c (lines 10–11);
4. d (lines 14–18); 5. b (lines 22–23); 6. b (lines 26–28);
7. d (lines 29–31)

Review Unit 4

Becoming an ACTIVE Reader

Expect students to activate prior knowledge, cultivate vocabulary, and think about meaning as they read. As they read, they should monitor their own reading habits and try to use effective strategies.

Fluency Reading: Billboards: Past and Present

Answer Key

Reading Comprehension:

1. c (lines 7–23); **2.** c (line 3); **3.** b (lines 4, 7–8); **4.** a (lines 18–19);
5. d (lines 22–23); **6.** c (lines 25–27); **7.** d (lines 27–29)

Self Check: Review of Reading Skills in Book 2

Personal Responses to Reading Strategy

Individual students will have different responses to the self check questions. The questions are meant to encourage reflection on the reading process. Students should use the questions in the Self Check to reflect upon their use of the reading strategies suggested throughout book 2.

Review Reading 7: The Life of a Food Critic

Answer Key

Reading Comprehension

1. c (line 6); **2.** b (lines 7–10); **3.** a (lines 12–13); **4.** d (lines 14–15); **5.** a (line 21); **6.** a (lines 23–25); **7.** d (lines 27–28)

Review Reading 8: Bringing Back the Aral Sea

Answer Key

Reading Comprehension

1. b (lines 1–2); **2.** a (lines 3–4); **3.** d (lines 9–11); **4.** c (lines 13–15);
5. c (lines 17–18); **6.** a (lines 22–23); **7.** d (lines 6–7, 23–26)

International Phonetic Alphabet (IPA)

Vowels

Symbol	Key Word	Pronunciation
/aː/	car	/kaː(r)/
/æ/	cat	/kæt/
/aɪ/	fine	/faɪn/
/aɪə/	fire	/faɪə(r)/
/aʊ/	house	/haʊs/
/aʊə/	our	/aʊə(r)/
/e/	bed	/bed/
/eɪ/	name	/neɪm/
/eə/	hair	/heə(r)/
/ɪ/	sit	/sɪt/
/iː/	need	/niːd/
/ɪə/	near	/nɪə(r)/
/ɒ/	hot	/hɒt/
/oʊ/	go	/goʊ/
/ɔː/	four	/fɔː(r)/
/ɔɪ/	toy	/tɔɪ/
/ʊ/	book	/bʊk/
/uː/	boot	/buːt/
/ʊə/	cure	/kʊə(r)/
/ɜː/	bird	/bɜː(r)d/
/ʌ/	cup	/kʌp/
/ə/	about	/əbaʊt/
/i/	very	/veri/

Consonants

Symbol	Key Word	Pronunciation
/b/	boy	/bɔɪ/
/d/	day	/deɪ/
/f/	face	/feɪs/
/g/	get	/get/
/h/	hat	/hæt/
/j/	yes	/jes/
/k/	car	/kaː(r)/
/l/	light	/laɪt/
/m/	my	/maɪ/
/n/	nine	/naɪn/
/p/	pen	/pen/
/r/	right	/raɪt/
/s/	see	/siː/
/t/	tea	/tiː/
/v/	vote	/voʊt/
/w/	west	/west/
/z/	zoo	/zuː/
/ʃ/	shoe	/ʃuː/
/ʒ/	vision	/vɪʒən/
/tʃ/	cheap	/tʃiːp/
/dʒ/	just	/dʒʌst/
/ŋ/	sing	/sɪŋ/
/θ/	think	/θɪŋk/
/ð/	they	/ðeɪ/

Coverage of TOEFL® iBT Reading Skills in ACTIVE Skills for Reading Book 2

Reading Purpose	TOEFL® iBT Skills Covered in Book 2
Reading to find information	Scanning for information: Units 2A, 2B, 4A, 7A, 12A
	Increasing reading fluency: Reviews 1–4
Reading for basic comprehension	Skimming for/Identifying main ideas: Units 5A, 6B, 8A, 10A
	Skimming to assess a passage: Unit 9A
	Using titles to understand main ideas: Unit 3A
	Identifying main ideas within paragraphs: Units 8A, 9B
	Making inferences: Unit 11A
	Finding Definitions: Unit 6A
	Predicting Vocabulary: Unit 5B
Reading to learn	Identifying cause and effect: Units 1B, 11B
	Recognizing sequence of events: Unit 3A
	Distinguishing main idea and supporting details: Units 1A, 10B